Professor Van Tongeren is one of the most important living psychologists studying religion and beliefs. His work details, with humility and sensitivity, why people abandon or change their religious beliefs, and he supportively offers suggestions about what residue might remain, and how people might rebuild community and meaning. This book is filled with research-based understanding and recommendations, and kindness.

–**ADAM B. COHEN, PhD,** PROFESSOR, DEPARTMENT OF PSYCHOLOGY,
ARIZONA STATE UNIVERSITY, TEMPE, AZ, UNITED STATES

An enlightening and compassionate resource, this timely book offers practical advice and profound insights for individuals reconstructing their religious beliefs or community. A blend of well-researched science and personal guidance for anyone on a journey of spiritual exploration and discovery.

–**CRYSTAL L. PARK, PhD,** PROFESSOR, PSYCHOLOGICAL SCIENCES,
UNIVERSITY OF CONNECTICUT, STORRS, CT, UNITED STATES

People's religious beliefs are central to their lives, yet in recent years so many people have been walking away from their faith. In this carefully researched yet deeply personal book, Van Tongeren explains why people typically leave their religions, and explores the diverse kinds of psychological reactions that people commonly experience after they leave. He offers an accessible and fascinating road map for what people can expect after they have left their religion behind them.

–**STEVEN J. HEINE, PhD,** PROFESSOR OF PSYCHOLOGY, UNIVERSITY OF
BRITISH COLUMBIA, VANCOUVER, BC, CANADA

T0246532

This book is a highly engaging and informative look at religious trauma, deconstruction, and creating the post-religious life. The crucial distinction Dr. Van Tongeren makes between religious "nones" and religious "dones" captures something so important, it should inform all subsequent research on this population. Both mental health professionals and people who have left high-control religions will find clear, research-based maps to the challenging and creative process of deconstruction in this important and helpful work.

–COCO OWEN, PhD, PSYCHOLOGIST IN PRIVATE PRACTICE, SPECIALIZING IN RELIGIOUS TRAUMA AND RECOVERY

I'm excited about this book, which I see as a go-to resource for anyone who has left religion or is struggling around such a decision. Packed with helpful psychological insights, relevant research findings, and practical suggestions, this book will also be useful for friends, family members, and therapists of those who pull away from religion.

–JULIE J. EXLINE, PhD, PROFESSOR, DEPARTMENT OF PSYCHOLOGICAL SCIENCES, CASE WESTERN RESERVE UNIVERSITY, CLEVELAND, OH, UNITED STATES

DONE

DONE

HOW TO FLOURISH
AFTER LEAVING RELIGION

DARYL R. VAN TONGEREN, PHD

 AMERICAN PSYCHOLOGICAL ASSOCIATION

Published by
APA LifeTools
750 First Street, NE
Washington, DC 20002
https://www.apa.org

Order Department
https://www.apa.org/pubs/books
order@apa.org

Typeset in Sabon by Circle Graphics, Inc., Reisterstown, MD

Printer: Sheridan Books, Chelsea, MI
Cover Designer: Mark Karis

Library of Congress Cataloging-in-Publication Data

Names: Van Tongeren, Daryl R., author.
Title: Done : how to flourish after leaving religion / Daryl R. Van
   Tongeren.
Description: Washington, DC : American Psychological Association, [2024] |
   Series: APA lifetools series | Includes bibliographical references and
   index.
Identifiers: LCCN 2024006098 (print) | LCCN 2024006099 (ebook) | ISBN
   9781433836237 (paperback) | ISBN 9781433841156 (ebook)
Subjects: LCSH: Psychology, Religious. | Conversion--Psychological aspects.
   | Uncertainty--Psychological aspects. | BISAC: SELF-HELP / Spiritual |
   PSYCHOLOGY / Psychotherapy / Counseling
Classification: LCC BL53 .V2834 2024 (print) | LCC BL53 (ebook) | DDC
   200.1/9--dc23/eng/20240515
LC record available at https://lccn.loc.gov/2024006098
LC ebook record available at https://lccn.loc.gov/2024006099

https://doi.org/10.1037/0000415-000

Printed in the United States of America

10 9 8 7 6 5 4 3 2 1

To Peter Boumgarden,
for modeling courageous curiosity,

and

Kevin Germer and Dave Stubbs,
for being steadfast and gracious companions
on my ongoing journey of religious change

Truths are illusions we have forgotten are illusions.
—Friedrich Nietzsche
On Truth and Lies in a Nonmoral Sense

CONTENTS

Acknowledgments   *xi*

Introduction: The Great Disillusionment   *3*

Chapter 1.   Why People Leave: The Four Horsemen   *17*

Chapter 2.   After Religious Trauma   *45*

Chapter 3.   Walking Away From Religion   *59*

Chapter 4.   Religious Residue   *85*

Chapter 5.   Searching for Meaning in the Existential Chasm   *105*

Chapter 6.   Crafting a New Identity   *139*

Chapter 7.   Navigating Relationships   *163*

Chapter 8.   Post-Religious Spirituality   *189*

Conclusion: Moving Forward   *207*

References   *209*

Index   *221*

About the Author   *227*

ACKNOWLEDGMENTS

I express my deep thanks to the many people who made this book a reality. Indeed, my research on religious change would still be an illusion in my own mind if not for Peter Boumgarden. I am grateful that he encouraged me to tackle a thorny research topic courageously. His continued encouragement and friendship have been lasting sources of joy and strength. The intellectual inspiration from our runs together is sufficient motivation to try to stay fit enough to keep pace with him.

Similarly, I am fortunate to collaborate with a host of smart, creative academics who are passionate about studying religion with cutting-edge scientific approaches. My sincere thanks to Nathan DeWall, who cowrote the primary grant proposal and was intricately involved in developing those studies and writing our papers. He helped me turn an idea into a reality and made it better in the process.

In the same vein, I thank Zhansheng Chen, Sam Hardy, Phil Schwadel, Julie Exline, Joe Bulbulia, Chris Sibley, Patty Van Cappellen, Aaron McLaughlin, Kelly Teahan, Cameron Mackey, Kim Rios, Donnie Davis, Ken Rice, Nick Stauner, David Bradley, Alex Uzdavines, and Ken Pargament, who coauthored papers from that project. I am fortunate to have such excellent collaborators. I extend my thanks to Isabella Brady for her work in assembling a literature review on religious change and deidentification. I am also grateful to the John Templeton Foundation for funding our grant proposal that produced this program of research on religious deidentification. My appreciation goes to Emily Ekle at APA Books for reaching out about this project and agreeing to give me enough time for the research to accumulate. I also thank her editorial team at APA Books for their incisive feedback.

Finally, I thank my wife, Sara, for our seemingly constant conversation about religious change. I can't count the number of contributions you've made to my thinking or insights you offered that have wholly changed how I think, or talk, about religion. This book is a product of more than a decade-long conversation over our shared meals, nature hikes, cross-country skiing, lakeside walks, fireside drinks, and intense intellectual deliberations. I am also grateful that you provided keen editorial feedback along the way, making the ideas and examples stronger and clearer. Your fingerprints are found throughout the pages in this book.

DONE

THE GREAT DISILLUSIONMENT

In 1927, Sigmund Freud published a critical analysis of religion, titled *The Future of an Illusion*. He viewed religion as a fictional illusion, born, in part, out of unconscious wish fulfillment. Although he acknowledged that religion had positive features, such as providing people with a moral framework and offering them a sense of meaning and purpose, he argued that it also had been used to oppress minoritized groups and keep certain folks in power. Instead, he called for people to move from religion to rationality, replacing these ancient beliefs with a secular set of sensibilities.

Now, roughly a century later, his book reads prophetic. The United States is experiencing the *Great Disillusionment*. People are leaving religion in the United States in staggering numbers. Although other parts of the Western world, such as Europe, have been becoming increasingly secularized for some time, and other regions in the world are still deeply religious (with Islam as the fastest growing religion worldwide outside the United States; Pew Research Center, 2015a), Americans are more recently walking away from their faith. We're living through a considerable change in the religious and cultural landscape.

Consider this: According to the Pew Research Center, over the past 30 years, the percentage of U.S. adults identifying as Christian has dropped from roughly 90% to 63% (Pew Research Center, 2022). The center is projecting that Christianity will no longer be the majority religion in the United States by 2070. By then, the number of religiously unaffiliated individuals would be roughly the same as Christians (if not slightly higher). On the whole, religious affiliation is on the decline, and across religions, younger generations are increasingly less likely to endorse religious beliefs and activities on numerous dimensions, including belief in God, heaven, hell, daily prayer, weekly religious service attendance, and the importance of religion in their lives (Pew Research Center, 2015b). This "rise of the nones" (i.e., people whose religious identity would be "none") includes a rise of people we call the "dones"—those who were once religious but no longer identify as such (Van Tongeren, DeWall, Chen, et al., 2021). Indeed, the overwhelming majority of nones (78%) were raised religious before walking away from their faith (Pew Research Center, 2016). In the United States, young adults raised Christian are decreasingly likely to convert to or remain Christian and increasingly likely to leave. Notably, Pew highlights that nearly one in three individuals raised Christian leave their faith by the time they reach age 30.

> *Religious nones: People whose religious identity would be "none."*
>
> *Religious dones: People who were once religious but no longer identify as such.*

I call this departure from religion the Great Disillusionment. Whereas the Great Awakening was a period of religious reignition and reengagement, what we're observing now is an exodus—still of the religious kind, but in a very different way. People are leaving churches, turning away from organized religion, and seeking alternative ways to engage with the transcendent. Some have estimated that nearly one in four Americans have switched religion (Public Religion Research Institute, 2023), and my own cross-cultural work suggests that the number of people leaving religion may be around one in five individuals (Van Tongeren, DeWall, Chen, et al., 2021). But with this disillusionment may come grief, loss, pain, and longing.

THE PANGS OF LOST FAITH

The shift has not come without costs: Many people are missing, if not longing for, experiences that only religion has uniquely provided. Many are looking for rituals, symbols, belonging, broader narratives of meaning, and an engagement with the mystical—features of human life that religion readily provided. As we'll come to see later in this book, we're naturally built to think and behave religiously, and as many collectively move away from traditional religious structures, the pangs of lost faith are real and pressing, and many are left searching for ways to address deep questions and seeking for lasting meaning. In turn, many have turned to alternative structures or practices as substitutes for divine relations.

As people depart from their religion, they often seek one of a few different paths. Some people are walking toward atheism, agnosticism, or unbelief. They've decided that their supernatural beliefs are misplaced, and they are squarely secular. Others may have expanded their religious beliefs, widened their perspective, or embraced doubt. They have grown and expanded, or perhaps experienced spiritual maturation. Still others are not satisfied with letting their spirituality languish. They are seeking out new ways to connect with the transcendent or experience deep existential meaning in ways that feel authentic. They haven't given up on their spirituality, just a religious identity that no longer fits. But one thing is clear: Many are also feeling a burgeoning sense of spiritual and existential dis-ease: They're anxious and

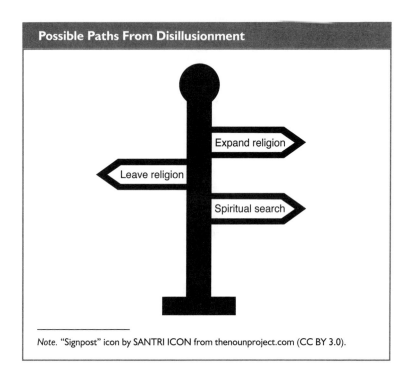

Possible Paths From Disillusionment

Expand religion ▶

◀ Leave religion

Spiritual search ▶

Note. "Signpost" icon by SANTRI ICON from thenounproject.com (CC BY 3.0).

unsettled, and some are seeking to satisfy the ancient longings religion once did.

Although no one can predict how long this Great Disillusionment will last—and what the final disposition of such a large-scale exodus from religious faith might be—it is clear that a substantial portion of Americans are experiencing religious change by leaving religion. Because we're in the middle of this shifting religious landscape, there are certainly more questions than answers about what the future might look like. But social scientists have shed some light on why people are leaving, where they are going, and how they might find meaning amid a changing religious identity.

This book is designed to help people who are either leaving or modifying their religion. In psychological terms, these two kinds of religious change are known as *religious deidentification* and *religious reconstruction*. Folks who leave religion undergo religious deidentification, and those who radically reshape their beliefs undergo religious reconstruction. And both start with a significant process called *religious deconstruction*, which is the usually lengthy (and often difficult) process through which people break down, analyze, question, and struggle with their religious worldview. As we'll see, the beginnings may look similar, but the destinations are quite different.

> *Religious deconstruction: The process of breaking down, analyzing, questioning, and struggling with one's religious worldview.*
>
> *Religious deidentification: The process of leaving one's religion altogether—toward atheism, agnosticism, or something else entirely that does carry a religious identity.*
>
> *Religious reconstruction: The process of rebuilding one's religious worldview into something that somewhat resembles one's original faith but diverges in important ways.*

Thus, this book will help not only those who have already left religion or are in the process of walking away, but also those who are still in the process of questioning their religious faith or tradition or actively working to rebuild it. Similarly, if you know or love someone who is undergoing religious change or want to know more about the process of leaving religion, this book explores the social and psychological processes involved.

In this book, I draw from the most relevant psychological theories and empirical scientific data. I discuss what we know and don't know about religious change, and I offer clear applications to help you build a life of meaning and flourishing. And I'll help those who still want to keep some parts of their spiritual life even though they are done with religion. By understanding other people who have left their religion, we can gain a better understanding of some of the deeper needs we humans share and how we address core questions about being human, understand how religion helped address these needs and questions, and look ahead to alternative ways of finding peace, engaging with the transcendent, and experiencing meaning.

YOU ARE NOT ALONE

In autumn 2019, I attended a gathering of people whose religious faith was changing. People from across the United States came together in community, unified by a singular commonality: Their old ways of being religious simply weren't working. My wife found this conference and recommended that we attend. In many ways, we were both experiencing rather significant shifts in our own religious and spiritual identities, and she thought this meeting would be interesting and potentially helpful. An old friend of mine from high school was driving to this event with his family from Kansas City, which just sweetened the experience.

I wasn't quite sure what to expect, and when we arrived, I was shocked at the popularity. Several thousand people were in attendance, many of whom shared the same story: They were raised as evangelical Christians and for myriad reasons no longer identified as such. Some in the crowd were still very interested in maintaining a spiritual life or connection to something greater. Others were wrestling with doubt and questions and weren't sure where they would land. Many, if not most, were angry and felt hurt by aspects of their religious upbringings. And some were completely finished with religion or anything to do with spirituality. I started brainstorming how better to understand this group more carefully and completely.

As I stood in the arena peering over the thousands of conference-goers, a singular thought overwhelmed me: *I am not alone.* Religious change can be a lonely experience. In predominantly religious cultures, walking away from religion can feel both terrifying and liberating, but it likely feels isolating. The reassuring news is that you are not alone. If you are in the process of rethinking your religious beliefs, have experienced religious loss or struggle, or have undergone a significant religious change, it's actually somewhat common— perhaps more common than you think. There are communities of people who have experienced similar things as you have. Of course, each of our journeys is unique and no one knows precisely what we've gone through, but a surprising number of people have decided to leave religion. And all of our very best estimates suggest that number is going to continue to increase.

I'll eventually unpack my own religious journey, but let me start with some comforting statistics. As a social psychologist, I've been studying the psychology of religion since my junior year project in college. But a conversation on a late autumn afternoon in 2017 changed the trajectory of my research in this area. My good friend Peter and I were sharing a 10-mile run to celebrate me turning in my materials for tenure and promotion. He asked, what was one thing I had been too afraid to study but would now like to pursue if granted the security of tenure. Without hesitation, I said "the process of leaving religion." With more nudging, I shared that it felt like a charged topic, an area ripe for discord. And, as someone who grew up deeply religious, it felt a bit unsettling to tackle. How could I breach this seemingly profane topic that felt like an affront to the way I was raised? Thanks to his encouragement, I decided to tack course, and since then, I've been deeply invested in studying religious change—how and why people change or leave religion.

A few months later, I wrote a grant proposal to study why people are leaving religion, and those funds supported a series of projects that help frame the research I discuss in this book. But one of our first discoveries was that one in five people report having left religion. That is, around 20% said that they formerly identified as religious but no longer do. So many researchers had been focusing on the "nones" that they largely ignored the *religious dones*—a group named as such because they are done with religion.

One in five.

I found this number rather surprising. When we were applying for the grant, my colleague and I had to make a case that there would actually be enough people leaving religion to make our efforts worthwhile. Our previous estimates used in our proposal, even at the most generous, would have put this number around 8% to 10%. When we saw the results come back at twice as high, we immediately knew that we were in an understudied but highly needed area of research. Since then, we've rather consistently seen in our U.S. samples that roughly a fifth of the respondents are religious dones.

If you are done with religion, this means that you're not alone. There are more people like you than you're probably aware. If you're not a religious done but your religious views are changing, you can take comfort in knowing that plenty of other people have gone through religious change, even if it looks different from yours.

These data fit into a larger sociological narrative that is unfolding in the United States and around the world: The number of people identifying as nonreligious is increasing (Pew-Templeton, 2015). More than 1.1 billion people in the world do not identify as religious, and that number is expected to grow by another 100 million. The upshot to this is that there is a community of people who do not identify as religious—and likely an even larger community of people who have undergone some kind of religious change. If this describes your experience, this book is for you.

THE BIG IDEA

This book is centered around one big idea: How can people who are no longer served by traditional religion craft a flourishing and meaningful life?

We'll tackle this big question in several ways. First, drawing from psychological science, I'll provide practical support and useful tips for people who are leaving religion. People are leaving church, or at least religion, in record numbers. In the United States, religious affiliation on the whole is declining, and we're especially seeing this among Christians—perhaps because Christianity has been the dominant religion, and perhaps because there are some sociocultural features that precipitated its decline. And among those who stay, many people's religious and spiritual beliefs are evolving in significant ways. For many of these individuals, a religious faith that once provided comfort, guidance, and an interpretative lens through which they can see the world no longer fits or feels authentic with their current beliefs and values. Many people are undergoing profound religious deconstruction. What predicts who experiences this religious evolution? How do people navigate this process? And what might suggest who retains their faith and who walks away? The psychological science I'll discuss integrates much of my own research on religious dones and research conducted by other leading scholars to provide a practical guide for people who are undergoing religious deconstruction or change.

Second, we'll look at the various expressions of religious deconstruction and deidentification and how this may play out in people's lives. The data on religious identity reveal that religious nones—or the religiously unaffiliated—are the third largest affiliative group in the world (Pew-Templeton, 2015). In a religion-saturated culture, and one that has primarily conflated religion and spirituality, it can be challenging to navigate the nuances of leaving religion.

Religious nones are a diverse group, including religious dones: those who were once religious but no longer identify as religious. Even among religious dones, the motivation for leaving religion varies, and their own personal beliefs and behaviors are unique. For some, this may mean abandoning one's beliefs; for others, it means leaving an institution that no longer fits them; and for others, it means letting go of a suddenly unhelpful or constricting label.

Finally, I hope to help individuals find new pathways to meaning and flourishing in the midst of, and following, this process. As this group is growing in size, research has only recently begun to accumulate. Because research in this area is relatively new, there hasn't been much work on establishing new pathways for flourishing or finding existential meaning. Religion leaves well-worn paths, and sometimes, effort is needed to find a new way. We'll also discuss how to address challenging social relationships with people who may not support, or understand, your process of religious deconstruction. This process can feel lonely and isolating, so we'll talk about the various ways to find connection and affirmation. And we'll explore the grief that can accompany the abandonment of religion and the autonomy that comes with finding a new way forward.

Here's an overview of how we're going to get there. First, we'll explore why people are leaving religion, and I'll give a little extra attention to the special case of religious trauma. We'll also examine what the process of walking away from religion involves and where people might end up. I'll introduce the concept of *religious residue*, which is where previous religious thoughts, feelings, and behaviors linger long after people have stopped identifying as religious—and how this shows up and might create unique challenges. We'll discuss how religion helps people make meaning that calms our existential concerns, so leaving religion can create an existential vacuum and leave people searching for new ways to make sense of their lives and the world around them. Next, we'll explore how to craft a new identity and navigate social relationships, especially among those who might not understand your religious changes. Finally, we'll discuss what spirituality after leaving religion might look like, as a way toward flourishing and hope.

THREE REQUESTS

For this book to be the most useful, I'll make three requests of you, the reader. First, I realize that not everyone reading this book comes from the same place, has the same view on religion, or will (or want to) end up at the same destination. Each of your experiences with religion is as unique as you are, so it'd be foolish to suppose that each of you will need the exact same things from this book. I understand that, and so I have tried to write with your religious diversity in mind. This means at some times, I may be speaking in generalities that don't apply to you or use terms with which you may no longer be comfortable. I've tried my best to be inclusive of the range of experiences you may bring to this book, and in the places I've misspoken or mischaracterized, I ask for your forgiveness, grace, and understanding.

Second, I know that for many, religion has been a source of pain or trauma. Some of you have experienced abuse at the hands of religious leaders or in the name of religion. Nothing can justify or excuse such horrors. I understand that religious hurts cut deeper than many other offenses, and spiritual pain is often complex and long-lasting. The process of leaving religion can be scary, isolating, or even dangerous, depending on your religious upbringing and current living situation. I take these considerations seriously and have tried to keep in mind those realities as I wrote. I am sensitive to the lasting wounds left by religion and have tried to offer empirically-based practical advice to navigating your transition away from religion. But there is often no replacement for therapeutic support. If you are a survivor of religious or spiritual trauma or abuse, I strongly recommend you seek support from a licensed mental health therapist who has experience working in this domain. It can be powerful, transformative, and healing. So, I also ask that you ensure you seek out a strong support network—friends, family (if possible), and professionals—as you navigate this transition. Finally, I ask you grant me the acknowledgment that a full understanding of religion requires nuance. Religion is neither the scourge of humanity nor the unblemished crown jewel of human culture. The truth is, religion is somewhere in between—religion has been a force for good and a source of considerable pain and prejudice. And because humans are messy and unpredictable, they interact with religion in myriad ways. I've adopted a scientific approach to examining religion, and the process of leaving religion, including what is good and freeing about it, as well as what is hard and tinged with grief. It's an emotionally and socially complicated process, and any authentically honest discussion of it will acknowledge this. So I ask that you embrace the tension of that difficult nuance.

Gathering together that each of you comes at this from your own unique history with different goals in mind, many of you have experienced significant pain at the hand of religion, and this topic requires holding the tension of nuance. Let's look at what science has to say about why people are leaving religion, what this process looks like, and how to craft a meaningful, flourishing life. Thank you for trusting me in this part of your journey. My hope is that this book will be a valuable and comforting companion.

ONWARD

The landscape of religion is changing. We're experiencing a Great Disillusionment as people are leaving religion. But just because religion no longer fits doesn't mean that we've stopped asking deep and enduring questions. We humans still wrestle with the existential concerns of what makes for a meaningful life, what happens to us after we die, and how to find connection with something larger than ourselves.

Some of us feel a void in the places where religion offered solace, whereas others feel anger and resentment toward religion in general. Some feel more authentic and free after having changed their beliefs, whereas others simply don't really think much about religion anymore. Wherever you are, we'll look at why religion is powerful, why it might be difficult to leave behind, and how to find freedom and flourishing after being disillusioned.

CHAPTER I

WHY PEOPLE LEAVE: THE FOUR HORSEMEN

In July 2019, Joshua Harris made a stunning announcement: He is an atheist. Although plenty of people don't believe in God, this public proclamation attracted considerable attention and controversy. Harris was the poster child for the Christian Evangelical purity movement. At age 21, he authored the best-selling *I Kissed Dating Goodbye*, which became the authoritative text on "pure" relationships within the Christian contexts. Elevated to near biblical status among adolescents in church pews across America, this volume detailed Harris's commitment to "courtship" rather than dating, with the intention of pursuing potential romantic partners for the sole purpose of determining their shared viability for marriage. Infused in these instructions on "godly relationships" were clear dictates for abstinence before marriage and the importance of maintaining sexual purity. His book, and indeed this countercultural alternative to romantic relationships, defined a generation of religious adolescents and young adults.

Harris seemingly had it all. He was successful and famous, a religious leader and public figure with influence and appeal. He had married his courted partner and had a lovely family. But something changed. Harris no longer believed. He could not make sense of his religious beliefs in light of his growth and change. He doubted—and ended up discarding—his entire worldview, which not only helped him make sense of the world but also helped him make his fame and fortune. In what can be perceived as a move toward acting with integrity with his values and new beliefs, Harris declared his new disbelief.

And that's not all that shattered for Harris. Accompanying his denouncement of the divine was his disclosure of his divorce, which, for many, was nearly equally egregious and damnable of an offense as his apostasy. His world was upended. And for many others, seeing a religious hero of their youth walk away from religion was deeply unsettling. If a pillar in the faith like Harris found his religious worldview intolerable and untenable, what might that mean for them? If *he* walked away, would they too? As evangelicals grappled to make sense of these events and the potential implications for their own lives, one thing was clear: In the end, Harris kissed *religion* goodbye.

BECOMING SECULAR

Why are people becoming disillusioned at all? What might account for these shifts in religious identification, and how can people make sense of their changing religious beliefs and identities?

Researchers have begun to advance the *secularization hypothesis*. This suggests that the world is moving beyond belief in the supernatural and is increasingly relying more on science and natural explanations. As technology, medicine, and society advance, perhaps belief in or reliance on supernatural agents wanes. Who needs a god to provide food or heal the sick, when you have the means to purchase food at a market or have access to a doctor who can prescribe medicine? Proponents of this idea point toward Europe and suggest that the United States will likely follow suit. Churches are treated a bit like museums—they are great places to visit, but they don't hold the same social influence in Europe as they do in America.

On the surface, this seems somewhat reasonable. Secularization in Europe might be spreading west, but this may not tell the whole story. It also doesn't fully explain why such an exodus is occurring. Such trends are not worldwide and may be more limited to developed countries with higher income and education. Other parts of the world are seeing strong religious engagement. In addition, when people leave religion, they may still want to believe in something more. Cultural advances in technology and medicine are helpful for improving the quality and duration of life but have little to offer in answering deep and enduring questions about what it means to be human. Existential questions around the meaning of life still persist.

Instead, I argue that there are four interlocking reasons people are leaving religion. I call these the *four horsemen of religion's apocalypse*, and they are ushering in the decline of religion (and perhaps most centrally, Christianity) in America. They better explain why secularization is happening, and why I predict we'll continue to see the vestiges of spirituality linger after this massive change in the religious landscape in the United States.

THE FOUR HORSEMEN OF RELIGION'S APOCALYPSE

Research on religious change and deconversion has been accumulating. Previous work has suggested reasons why people might leave. For example, some researchers have argued that some have intellectual struggles with their faith, whereas others experience suffering (Barbour, 1994; Streib, 2012, 2021). Other empirical work revealed that people leave because of how the church treats LGBTQ+ individuals (Flanery, 2022), suggesting a cultural mismatch. Still other work has revealed that the label of religious, or "evangelical" in particular, is problematic (State of Theology, 2022). More recently, scholars have examined people deconverting (Bullivant, 2022) or leaving church

(J. Davis et al., 2023). Together, this work began to assemble a collection of reasons why people are leaving religion.

Building on this work, my colleagues and I tried to categorize the primary reasons people are leaving religion. Specifically, we sampled more than 100 people, asking them to write in detail about why they left their faith (McLaughlin et al., 2022). Then, I and another research team member coded all of the written essays, looking for common themes, many of which dovetail with other research (Wright et al., 2011). Although each person's story is unique, they suggest there may be four rather similar trajectories that may lead people to leave religion, each representing one of the four horsemen prophesying doom for religion:

- *Cultural stagnation*—many people report undergoing a progressive shift (e.g., outgrowing their religion), including people who were raised in conservative religious homes but have become more liberal and progressive over time and no longer feel as though their beliefs "fit";
- *Religious trauma*—many others report a traumatic exit from religion (e.g., pointing to religious trauma), including those people who suffered a personal or religious trauma and no longer want to be associated with religion or religious individuals;
- *Simplistic views of suffering*—some reported unresolved suffering (e.g., indicated they experienced significant adversity) and were unable to make sense of personal adversity or suffering in light of what they had been taught about God or the divine; and
- *A problematic label*—some described leaving religion because they did not want that identity label or because of social pressure (e.g., a community that was unwelcoming or a partner who was nonreligious).

We'll explore each of these reasons in more detail.

The Four Horsemen of Religion's Apocalypse

1. Cultural stagnation
"I have learned and evolved, and my religion no longer reflects my values or understanding of the world."

2. Religious trauma
"My religion caused me or others harm."

3. Simplistic views of suffering
"My religion can't adequately explain why life is cruel and unfair."

4. The problematic label
"I don't agree with what 'religion' stands for anymore" or "I'm not like other religious people."

Note. "Knight" icon by Hey Rabbit from thenounproject.com (CC BY 3.0).

The First Horseman: Cultural Stagnation

Our data strongly suggested that cultural stagnation is a primary reason for leaving religion (McLaughlin et al., 2022). The first, and largest, group of participants from our study reported intellectual reasons for leaving religion or mentioned that they "outgrew" their faith. They mentioned things such as choosing science and facts over religion or outgrowing their faith once they were a reasonable adult who could think for themselves. More than half of the participants from our data gave this explanation for their religious exit. Notably, many reported a difference between the faith they were raised in and what they believe now. This intellectual reasoning for leaving religion represents a progressive shift in the face of religion's cultural stagnation: moving away from the conservative religious beliefs of one's upbringing toward a broader, and now irreligious, worldview. And it underscores that many religious beliefs and teachings are culturally antiquated or directly at odds with other aspects of people's ideology.

As people learn and grow, you may expect different aspects of their attitudes and beliefs to grow as well. When I attended college, my world expanded. Not only did I learn new things, but I had to unlearn some of the things I was wrongly taught before. Some of this is developmentally appropriate because we can't fully grasp the abstract concepts of complex ideas at earlier ages. But other things I learned were in direct opposition to my religious upbringing. How could I reconcile some seemingly inconsistent facts about the world in which I lived or how humans process information with religious teachings from my youth? For many of us, it's a process of sorting which religious beliefs to hold on to, which to revise, and which to discard.

But this process isn't only for scientific facts or knowledge about the physical world. It's also for attitudes and beliefs. Many people begin to question whether some of the foundational things they were taught about gender and sexuality, how relationships are supposed to work, and who should be in power are actually aligning with other things they are learning. A substantial number of people walk away from Christianity because of a lack of acceptance, and perhaps outright exclusion and derogation, of the LGBTQ+ community, its views of women and racial and ethnic minorities, the predominance of patriarchy, or its restrictive views on gender and sexuality. The range of beliefs espoused within this particular framework—including sexism, patriarchy, purity culture, white supremacy, mistrust of science, forms of intolerance—are being challenged by those who no longer want to ascribe to a narrowing set of beliefs that excludes and harms others (including themselves). Those who have engaged in significant intellectual wrestling likely may now be more affirming and inclusive on this and other aspects of social life. As people have more diverse experience and gain more cultural knowledge, they may begin to see their religion as being outdated at best or, at worst, causing more social harm than good.

How might the progressive shift in response to cultural stagnation look? For many, this process is gradual. Few people have radical deconversions where they suddenly decide to stop being religious. It may more closely resemble a years-long process of evolving beliefs. As one friend put it, he kept moving further and further down the bench until he realized that he was no longer seated at the table of Christianity. He didn't plan on leaving. But as he changed and grew, his beliefs changed and grew, and over time he realized, he could no longer identify as a Christian. To do so would be inauthentic. For others, as they progress through education; learn more about the way the world works; and perhaps start careers in science, technology, or medicine, some of the beliefs they were taught growing up come into conflict with newly learned knowledge. For example, being taught that Earth was created in six literal days and is no more than 10,000 years old stands in stark contrast to scientific evidence suggesting the universe is billions of years old, and the star in the night sky whose light is reaching your eye is several million light years away, which makes such "young Earth" math impossible. And while some people were taught the cognitive gymnastics to make such thinking consonant (e.g., God created the world to appear old although it is quite young and recent), eventually the cracks in those beliefs become too much, and people start to question their beliefs. If the doubting and questioning is not sufficiently resolved, they may leave their faith. Religions that cannot adapt to cultural demands may not survive.

The Second Horseman: Religious Trauma

The second most commonly reported reason for leaving faith was because of religious trauma. Religious trauma is a nefarious culprit causing people to leave religion. Individuals reported the hypocrisy among the church members as a primary reason for departure. For some, this looked like the sexual abuse scandals that rocked many congregations (including the large-scale scandal of abusive priests in the Catholic Church and evangelical leaders like Hillsong), whereas others reported trauma related to being persecuted by religious leaders for identifying as LGBTQ+. Horrifically, and all too commonly, some mentioned being told explicitly by a pastor that they were going to hell for being gay. This group left religion through a traumatic exit: After experiencing religious and spiritual trauma, these individuals walked away from the faith that caused them so much pain. This is often one of the most emotional and challenging departures from religion.

People may report religious trauma for a number of reasons. It may be because they hold an identity (e.g., sexual orientation, gender expression, political orientation, ethnicity) that is derogated, mar-ginalized, or condemned by church teachings. Perhaps they suffered abuse by a controlling leader who manipulated them emotionally or psychologically. Others may have been coerced or misled into giving their money, time, or professional talents to a cause they no longer believe in. Some may have radically altered their behavior based on teachings from the pulpit, such as abstaining from sexual activity, only later to find out that the pastor regularly had illicit sexual encounters with parishioners. Still, some see the mismatch between religious teachings (e.g., loving all people) and the behavior of religious individuals (e.g., judging and ostracizing those who believe differently) and find this hypocrisy an insurmountable barrier to religion and evidence for its inauthenticity. In short, there are many places religious trauma or abuse may have emerged while being religious.

This traumatic exit following religious trauma and abuse may happen suddenly or gradually. And it may take time to uncover that one's exit from religion was indeed traumatic. For example, some may be fed up with trying to justify their existence, dignity as a person, and worth as a human, after being told who they are is a sin and decide to leave their religious community and faith altogether. After all, if you are consistently told that God hates who you are, why believe in such a punitive and judgmental supernatural being? Others may point to a specific event, such as a religious leader's admission to immoral behavior or when church officials are caught behaving in unscrupulous ways, as the "straw that broke the camel's back" and instigated their departure from a hypocritical institution. Surely, there is often considerable hurt and pain associated with a traumatic exit.

Yet for some, they may not fully realize the severity of the trauma of their religious experiences until some time after leaving. Those raised in more restrictive faiths, in which teachings forbade certain activities around sex, food, or fun, may reflect on perceived losses in their upbringing and grieve not only how those teachings precluded them for engaging in a life they may have wanted but also may have guided their behavior toward decisions they may not have otherwise made. For example, those raised in purity culture—which is the set of religious teachings that women must remain sexually "pure" and

25

abstinent until marriage—may lament a lack of sexual experiences in adolescence, harbor resentment for feeling enduring shame for having had various sexual experiences, or may feel contempt for having gotten married at a young age as the one route toward sexual fulfillment, only later to wonder how life would have been different if they would have only had sex with rather than marry their current partner. They may later see these experiences as traumatic, largely fueling their exit from their faith. In the next chapter, we'll devote more time to exploring this reason for leaving religion, as well as discuss some resources for support if this describes your experience.

The Third Horseman: Simplistic Views of Suffering

A third, common reason why people leave their faith is because of religion's simplistic views of suffering. In the United States, the rise of overly positive views of religion and spirituality and the "prosperity gospel" of some strands of American Evangelicalism have left religious adherents ill-equipped for navigating the suffering inherent in life. We could also call this "toxic positivity," but the idea is that many religions offer simple accounts for human life that cannot fully explain the cruelty of human suffering. On the flipside, some religious traditions simply blame the faithful for their hardship. Indeed, nearly 15% reported personal adversity as their primary rationale for walking away from their religion (McLaughlin et al., 2022). Nearly all such respondents indicated the death of a loved one or unanswered prayers as a central source for this suffering. For example, one respondent shared that the death of their friend when they were both children drove them away from religion. Surely, they reason, how could a loving God allow an innocent child to perish? Others shared about a sick relative for whom they prayed for God to heal, only to have their loved one suffer in anguish until they died. One shared about the indignant way a loved one died after a long struggle, during which God felt absent.

Suffering poses a significant problem for many people's religious beliefs. For many, experiencing suffering is an obstacle in maintaining religious beliefs and practices. A central issue revolves around how people make sense of the problem of evil—what scholars call *theodicy*. Put simply, many people believe that God is (a) all-powerful (omniscient), (b) all-knowing (omniscient), and (c) all good (omnibenevolent). If this is the case, then how can evil, sin, or sickness pervade the world? Why do bad things happen at all? Suffering calls into question these assumptions: Is God not very powerful and simply powerless to stop this evil? Does God allow these bad things to happen? Or is God not all-knowing? Perhaps God is trying to figure things out like we are. Or, perhaps most unnerving, is that God may not be all good. Could it be the case that God actually causes these bad things to happen? Is this part of a cruel joke or sick test? Any of these considerations is deeply unsettling to the way most people think about God. After all, most people hold a view that God is good, loving, and powerful. How, then, do people make sense of unanswered prayers and the death of loved ones who seemed undeserving of an indignant end to their life?

A related problem comes from our pervasive belief in a just world. This belief is commonly embedded in religious teachings, and the belief in a just world is summarized thusly: People get what they deserve (Lerner & Lerner, 1980). Good things happen to good people, and bad things happen to bad people. Overall, this belief holds that life is fair. When suffering strikes, especially those who we consider innocent and relatively powerless, such as children, it upends our view of a just world. Things don't make sense. We argue that they didn't deserve it. And when bad things happen to us, we're left with a tough choice: Are we not as good as we thought we were (i.e., did we do something to deserve this?) or is the world more chaotic, unpredictable, and unfair than we imagined? Either consideration is anxiety-provoking, because the former leaves us blaming ourselves and heaping on the guilt and shame to maintain some notion of cosmic justice, where that latter means a considerable part of how we think the world works is mistaken, and the world is far more uncertain and chaotic than we care to admit.

Any number of sources of suffering can trigger a period of religious *deconstruction* (i.e., breaking down, analyzing, questioning, and struggling with one's core religious beliefs) because such experiences undermine people's sense of meaning and violate what so many people have been taught about religion. And the suffering doesn't even have to be personal; we might be cast into existential turmoil by trying to make sense of widespread famine, systemic oppression, or the slow but steady impending climate crisis. But both personal and social tragedies often affect how people engage with religion and how they view God (e.g., God's omnipotence, role in human lives, control, benevolence, authoritarianism). Sometimes religion can help us navigate this suffering. Buddhism, for example, assumes that suffering is an inherent part of life and offers suggestions for how to navigate this suffering. Other times, religion exacerbates our suffering, and people feel the only authentic move is to jettison their religious beliefs that are simply ineffective in dealing with the reality of their suffering. There is other research on how to navigate seasons of suffering, but research suggests that for many, suffering ushers in a crisis of faith (Van Tongeren & Showalter Van Tongeren, 2020).

When religion promises easy answers to avoid or overcome suffering, it often causes more harm than good. Many religions would do better to embrace the messiness and nuance of suffering or to admit that suffering remains a persistent, and perhaps unexplainable, problem. But often, religious leaders double down. Perhaps a religious leader blamed someone for their suffering, condemning them for bringing it on themselves for (hidden) sin in their life. Or they might tell the afflicted simply to have more faith or pray harder; a lack of a positive result is due to one's feeble faith. Someone may have been told that God uses everything for good, which leads people to conclude that God must have an odd, or twisted, view of goodness if miscarriages, childhood cancer, or sudden and tragic deaths of parents of young children are somehow painted as good. After my brother died tragically at age 34, with three children under age 6, someone told me that God needed my brother in heaven more than the world needed him. To me, it sure seemed that his children would have appreciated having a loving and selfless father for a few more decades while God could get by waiting a bit longer. It makes it hard to feel loved by that kind of God and, if anything, makes God seem selfish.

The Fourth Horseman: The Problematic Label

The term religion has taken on new meanings in the United States. And for many, these meanings are quite problematic. The last portion of our respondents, just over one tenth of the participants, indicated social reasons for leaving their faith—highlighting that religion may have a problematic label. Many respondents indicated that they did not agree with the politics infused into religion. Others plainly reported that they didn't like the label, for some because it was becoming too complicated, and for others because it now felt uncomfortable to be labeled as religious. They no longer "fit" as religious. Some of this misfit may have come from social influence, such as marrying a partner who was not religious or moving away from a religious family or community. But some even noticed that when a local religious community was unwelcoming, they no longer wanted to be religious. The thrust here is that people no longer feel like they align with whatever "religion" has become. And they want out.

In the United States, particularly after 2016, "evangelical" became an increasingly politicized term. After 81% of White, born-again evangelical Christians voted for Donald Trump in the presidential election, evangelical carried a different connotation. Those who had long identified as evangelical but did not agree with or endorse the actions of Trump or his political allies suddenly wanted to distance themselves from that problematic label. Even those who might have voted for him but soured on his policies or behavior may have denounced that moniker and decided to walk away, into something else. On the other hand, those who were politically aligned with this new brand of conservative politics may have adopted the label. A poll in 2022 revealed that more than 40% of evangelicals do not believe in Jesus as God (State of Theology, 2022). Considering the deity of Jesus has been a central tenet (if not the central tenet) of evangelicalism since its inception, it begs the question of what, precisely, this term has come to mean in the minds and hearts of Americans. So, for those who might still want to engage spiritually but no longer find resonance with that label or want to be associated with those who do, an exit seems like the only option.

When a religion comingles its identity with strong, divisive groups (like certain political alliances), it can isolate large portions of its followers. Especially as politics have played an increasingly outsized role in religion in the United States, including primarily Christian Evangelicalism, many religious adherents feel as though they don't fit and no longer want to "hitch their wagons" to the horse that is leading them in a direction with which they disagree. Some consider their religious "baggage" simply to be too much, and they want to free themselves from the label that comes with social implications and implicit connotations. Even if religious means one thing to you, it can mean many other things to other people. If you ask 12 people what religion means, you'll probably get 19 answers, and some people will still disagree with all of the responses. Because it's hard to control the impression that other people have of us if they find out that we're religious, some people avoid that altogether and leave the label behind. They see it as more problematic than beneficial (or accurate).

For others, leaving the label is a brave act of autonomy. To them, if being religious means being racist, sexist, homophobic, xenophobic, or otherwise exclusionary, then, no, they are not religious at all. They refuse to participate in a system that seems light-years away from the central messages of love and humility on which many religions were based. People may realize that the label is less and less necessary—or descriptive. A shifting meaning of the word religion can drive people away and help explain why people are leaving religion.

WHAT ALL FOUR HORSEMEN HAVE IN COMMON: COGNITIVE DISSONANCE

Each of these narratives is different and there are likely other reasons not captured in this tidy list. Certainly, some people may report multiple reasons for leaving religion. Yet these four trajectories converge on a central psychological mechanism: They are all partly about cognitive dissonance. The way people thought that the world works no longer lines up with reality or makes sense with their beliefs.

Cognitive dissonance is the uncomfortable feeling people have when there is an inconsistency between their beliefs and their behaviors (Festinger, 1957). This major social psychological theory has explained how people deal with internal contradictions or discrepancies between what people think and do. For example, when people know smoking is harmful to their health but continue to smoke anyway, they probably experience some degree of dissonance. When our attitudes and actions don't align, we're motivated to eliminate this feeling, and we have a few options to do so. One way can do this is by changing our attitude about smoking in general, such as arguing whether the results of smoking studies were actually conclusive. Or we could think of supporting evidence for our behavior, such as reminding ourselves that Grandpa smoked two packs of cigarettes per day and lived to be 95. We could justify, rationalize, or downplay our behaviors by saying that smoking actually relieves our stress so is good for us, or we don't smoke that much, or we're planning on quitting soon anyway. Or we could change our behavior, which often feels like the last option because doing so takes quite a bit of work, and we often wait until it is unbearably uncomfortable.

> *Cognitive dissonance: The uncomfortable feeling people have when there is an inconsistency between their beliefs and behaviors.*

In the reasons people offered for why they left religion that we just discussed, the dissonance doesn't come as a result of some behavior like smoking, but rather because of how our beliefs collide with reality. And there's little we can do to change reality; but we can change our relationship with reality. We often twist or distort reality to bend the facts in ways that align with our beliefs. This is pretty common. We like to make sense of the world in ways that match well with our expectations. This process, called *assimilation*, may look like us going along with religion for longer than feels initially comfortable. We make things fit into our religious frameworks, or schemas, because once we do, the discomfort dissipates. For example, we make excuses for a religious leader's poor behavior by saying he was tempted by the devil, double down on how scientific evidence can't overpower the inerrancy of the Bible, or tell ourselves that despite the senselessness of the death of a friend's child, God's plan is bigger and better, although we privately don't know just how or why. Our initial pangs of doubt and inconsistency are quickly assuaged by this assimilative process.

However, there are some situations when we simply cannot fit our experiences into our existing cognitive frameworks. In these cases, through a process called *accommodation*, we have to change what we believe. Our religious schemas may be tweaked, or they may be shattered. It depends on how discrepant the experience was. If you think God is all-loving and has blessed you with a prosperous life and you lose several family members in a tragic car accident at the same time, chances are that your beliefs about God and how the world works suddenly need a major overhaul. You may not be able to fit something like that into your existing schema. You have to change your beliefs.

For individuals undergoing a progressive shift due to religion's cultural stagnation, perhaps they have experienced changing beliefs and intellectual growth that renders their previous religious beliefs

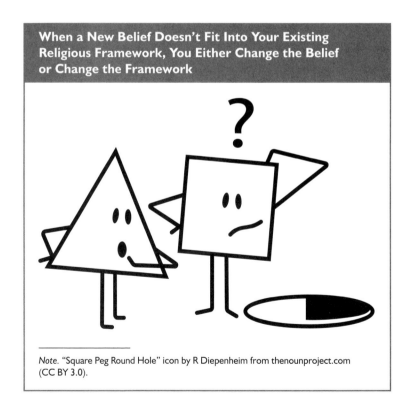

When a New Belief Doesn't Fit Into Your Existing Religious Framework, You Either Change the Belief or Change the Framework

Note. "Square Peg Round Hole" icon by R Diepenheim from thenounproject.com (CC BY 3.0).

ill-fitting, or they seek to be spiritual but not religious. They were unable to integrate their religious beliefs with new knowledge as they grew, changed, and learned more. Something had to give, and religion went.

Those who left religion because of a trauma may be reeling from the fallout and trying to make sense of a world in which their worldview and personal sense of safety has been violated. Their trust in religion, religious leaders, and God may have been shattered as they try to align what happened to them with how they deserved to be treated. They may be seeking healing in a place that is safer and more welcoming.

For those who left because religion could not help them make sense of their suffering, their expectations of the world (and God) did not match, and they could not make sense of their tragedy or adversity. Their beliefs are inconsistent with their experiences. Religion may have made their suffering worse, so they decided to stop trying to engage in the mental gymnastics necessary to explain the role of a seemingly angry, absent, or uncaring God in allowing or causing indescribable pain in their lives.

And for those who leave the problematic religious label behind, what they thought religion meant is not aligning with the social experience of religion. They do not want to be associated with a religious group that has been the source of so much hurt. Here, too, thoughts and behaviors did not align, and religion was the source of this troubling inconsistency.

The departure from religion may be, in part, a way of managing our cognitive dissonance. What we were taught no longer holds up to the scrutiny of life, and we need to bring our attitudes and behaviors into alignment with the reality of our experiences. Make no mistake, this process is painful. It's discomforting, disorienting, and downright frightening at times. After all, if religion was a central part of your identity and a primary way by which you made sense of the world, to walk away from religion is a bit like walking away from yourself—or at least a version of yourself. At least at first, many people struggle to forge an identity apart from their religion. Many feel guilt and shame, which are common emotions associated with religion. Others feel considerable fear about being wrong in their new beliefs, especially given that fear has often been a reliable tool of persuasion in religion. And in leaving, some may (also) feel freedom, authenticity, and agency. It can feel at once like the best and the most terrifying decision of their life. And it may be one that they second-guess.

All of this is normal. In fact, some of it might be part of a developmental process. We all form schemas, or cognitive frameworks, as a normal part of human development (Piaget, 1953). As we grow and mature, we can reason differently, so we revise and update our schemas based on new information. Whenever possible, we fit information from the world into our schemas so that everything makes sense. But when there is too great of a mismatch between our experiences and our beliefs, we have to change what we believe. This cognitive developmental process extends into our understanding about religion and faith as well (Fowler, 1981; Fowler & Dell, 2006). As we learn more about the world and how to think and reason differently, our religious beliefs change and grow as well. For some, this looks like faith maturation; for others, this may look like leaving religion. More recently, scholars have argued that questioning may simply be part of any maturation of faith or spiritual development (Jones, 2023). Of course, there are factors that may lead some folks to leave while others remain.

RECENT SUPPORT FOR THE FOUR HORSEMEN

One recent study polled more than 1,000 ex-Christians to find out their motivations for leaving their faith (Flanery, 2022). The results align well with my theory of the four horsemen. In the study, the author asked six open-ended questions and coded the themes in the responses. Two results were particularly illuminating. First, most people leaving left Christianity altogether—either toward atheism, agnosticism, or something else entirely, with only around 10% identifying with as a different type of Christian. (That type of movement is probably akin to *reconstruction*, where people break down their beliefs and rebuild them into something that resembles their original faith but diverges in important ways.) So the shift we're seeing in people walking away from religion is not merely a linguistic exercise. Most of the religious dones have truly left their faith. The Great Disillusionment is not a mirage.

Second, when asked why they left, more than a fifth of the respondents of this particular poll reported it was due to the church's discrimination of LGBTQ+ individuals (Flanery, 2022). Notably, the author conducting this poll indicated that a substantial portion of those completing the survey were sexual minorities, but this concern was widespread and led to many individuals doubting their faith. This aligns with my central hypotheses for two of the four horsemen: Many conceptualizations of religion are failing to meet the needs of the evolving cultural pressures, and, for many, this is creating a mismatch that cannot be easily reconciled, brought on by cultural stagnation and religious trauma at the hands of the church. Other powerful reasons for walking away include the hypocritical actions of religious individuals and the role of politics in religion. The author speculated that conflating evangelicalism and pro-Trump Republicanism was a deciding factor that drove many away. Indeed, the religious label was problematic. Political and cultural pressures are real and are often intermixed with deeply held religious beliefs.

But this demonstrates a larger point: Expressions of religion that cannot account for the social demands of a culture are likely going to struggle to gain, and retain, followers. Research shows that many people who leave religion think the church is out of touch on key social and cultural issues (Reyes et al., 2021). However, this process is not always a death sentence. There may always remain a small group of adherents for whom the departure of the disaffected and disillusioned intensifies their commitment and serves to prove that those walking away are false prophets, and those who remain are the true, chosen, and elect. Viewing the outside culture as a threat can lead to stronger commitment, as people double down in steadfast belief that they must protect their religious worldview more vigorously and staunchly than ever before. Only with vigilance can such an attack be thwarted. As a result, those remaining in such a religious faith may shift even more ardently toward those very values that led to the departure of previously religious individuals. And as these religious dones look back, the gap between who they are and who they were looks bigger—in part, because the gap now is bigger. Those that are left are more extreme in their views—and potentially getting more extreme by each passing moment.

WHO LEAVES AND WHO STAYS?

Although the Four Horsemen aren't exhaustive, they are rather comprehensive. By that, I mean most religious people may confront one of these four reasons at some point in their life. Everyone grows up, but not everyone outgrows their religion (Jones, 2023). In fact, some people find religion later in life. Older people are more religious than younger individuals, although some (but not all) of this may be due to generational differences (Bengtson et al., 2015). Most people were made aware of the sexual abuse scandal in the Catholic Church, but plenty of people remain Catholic. Others have witnessed leaders act reprehensibly, and some have been treated terribly by pastors or clergy, and they remain committed followers and regular service attenders. Eventually, everyone experiences suffering or personal adversity, but the rate of religion doesn't bottom-out at zero. Plenty of folks remain, and many rely on their religious beliefs to provide them comfort when life is challenging. And people move in and out of social settings where religion is more or less prioritized, yet plenty of people remain steadfastly committed to their religious identity regardless of their surroundings. Labels change and take on evolving meanings, and many people actually prefer the current meaning of religious labels in the United States.

How can we make sense of all of this? Are people who leave religion simply more enlightened and aware than those who are ostensibly mindless and following religion without critically thinking? Are those who leave religion weaker than those who stay committed to their faith? Is it a crapshoot, with no better odds than a roulette wheel in Vegas?

We all have experiences with these reasons for potential departure. Although work in this area is still new, there are a few clues about who stays and who leaves religion. First, one predictor might be the degree of the discrepancy people experience between their beliefs and reality. Extreme tragedy, such as the death of a spouse or child, may jar people out of their religious worldviews because they cannot make sense of how a loving God could allow or would cause that to happen. Similarly, survivors of physical or sexual abuse may question God's absence during their suffering or the lack of justice for their abusers. Such heartbreak violates some of the deepest held beliefs about God and assumptions about the way the world works. And because reality has this pesky way of showing up in our consciousness unless we succumb to our elaborate defensive mechanisms to deny, distort, or dissociate from it, eventually we must reckon with the harsh, cruel, cold, and seemingly uncaring way that world (and death) takes and takes and takes, and make an account for where God might be amid this ongoing theft of life. Put simply, the greater the discrepancy between how we thought the world was going to be and how God was supposed to act, and the way the world actually is, the more distress we feel and the more stress it puts on how we make meaning out this adversity (Park, 2010). In many such extreme cases, our assumptions, and faith, are shattered.

In a similar vein, a second predictor of who leaves their faith behind may be the severity of trauma someone endures. Although any trauma is horrid, unjust, and inexcusable, those who experienced a more severe or complex trauma may be more likely to walk away from religion. Our bodies and minds are designed to remember threats so we can avoid them, and similar other threatening situations, in the future. Traumatic events are often seared into our minds, leaving our brains to play them on repeat to try to steer us away from future pain and toward safety. They also affect how we think, act, and react to situations. Abuse at the hands of religious individuals, institutions, or leaders may lead many rightfully to want to avoid any intimation of religion as a means to caring for their own psychological well-being and emotional and physical health. Staying in an abusive or traumatic situation, when one can leave safely, can lead to prolonged pain, so when people are able to leave religion, they may do so and never want to go back. Comparing trauma is rarely helpful, but those who personally experienced trauma and abuse may be more motivated to leave than those who were made aware of abuses within in their congregation or religious community. I'd highly recommend that anyone who has experienced religious abuse or trauma seek out a mental health therapist trained to address this complex issue for support in working toward healing and wholeness.

A third predictor of who leaves the faith may be the style of belief an individual has. Consider two kinds of religious believers. One holds their beliefs rigidly. They have a high degree of certainty, and there is little (if any) room for negotiation. They're pretty convinced that they are right and can surely dispatch challenges to their faith. The other holds their beliefs more flexibly. Their religious beliefs may shift when they encounter questions or experience doubt. They're not completely sure they are right. Who do you think would be more likely to leave the faith?

Many suspect the rigid dogmatist can withstand the onslaught of opposition to their faith. And in the short term, they're right. They do pretty well overcoming the little bumps in the road. But when something bigger comes along, they're often unable to account for this change, and may toss out their faith wholesale. Many learning about evolution as a compelling scientific alternative to what they were taught may then assume that everything they've previously learned is wrong and must be discarded. They reason, "If I can't know everything, I must not know anything." Rather than throw the baby out with the bathwater, those who hold their beliefs more flexibly can withstand some larger threats or challenges. They can absorb this pressure in a "bend-but-not-break" style of faith. They can alter features of their religious beliefs without giving up on the whole of their religion. They may operate with a bit more uncertainty than the rigid believer, but they may also be less likely to leave when facing a seemingly insurmountable obstacle to their faith.

Related to this, a fourth predictor may be personality or demographic features. Research has found that men are more likely to walk away from religion than women are (Reyes et al., 2021). Research on personality is a bit mixed. There is some research that suggests people who are open to new experiences and are more likely to seek novelty may be more likely to leave religion (McCrae, 1999). Compared with those who remain in their religion, openness to new experiences was considerably higher (i.e., one standard deviation) for those who left (Streib et al., 2009). But other work suggests that this personality characteristic is not a consistent predictor (Streib, 2021; Stronge et al., 2021). More consistently, other work suggested that neuroticism was associated with leaving religion (Saroglou, 2020). Indeed, correlational and longitudinal work has shown that emotional instability is associated with walking away from one's faith (Chen et al., 2022; Streib et al., 2009). It is possible that those who are high on agreeableness (i.e., prioritize getting along with others) and conscientiousness (i.e., are highly attuned to order and following the rules) may be more likely to stay in religion, compared to those for whom these features of personality are less salient (Saroglou, 2010, 2017). Longitudinal work has revealed decreases in agreeableness before deconversion (Stronge et al., 2021). Taken together, this work might suggest that those who demonstrate more emotional variability and are less motivated by conformity and tradition may be especially likely to leave religion (Saroglou et al., 2020). So, if you've regularly been someone who has pushed the boundaries and roiled against convention, given the right circumstances, you might find yourself primed to walk away from your faith.

I also expect that these different features interact with one another. For example, someone who was raised in an extremely religiously fundamentalist environment that mandated a rigid and inflexible faith would experience rather severe discrepancy between the beliefs and their upbringing and their new view of the world. In addition, upon reflection, they may identify that part of how the group maintained its control and membership was for the religious leaders to act in manipulative and emotionally abusive ways. For many, this may lead to particularly strong exits, which are even more pronounced for people who integrated much of this polarized thinking of their religious upbringings into their cognitive style. The result may be a shattered faith, a complete denouncement of any form of religion, and significant emotional pain (and lingering effects of trauma) surrounding religion or religious individuals.

TAMING THE HORSEMEN

It's important to understand how this research can help you in your process of leaving religion. In practice, what does all this mean for you? And how can this knowledge support your crafting a flourishing life? Here are a few places to start:

- **Reflect on your reasons.** First, you might locate yourself in one of these stories of deidentification. Consider the reason, or reasons, why you left religion. What were the most significant areas of pain, challenge, or loss? There may be several ways in which you've experienced a struggle with religion, so it can be helpful to clarify a few key driving factors. If you find resonance with one of the reasons, it can help remind you that you're not alone. If your reasons are different, don't worry—each person's departure from religion is unique, and plenty of people don't fit neatly into these categories.

- **Examine your beliefs.** As you reflect on your rationale for departing, you may want to ask yourself in what ways did your experiences challenge your previous beliefs about how you thought the world worked? Where were the inconsistencies in your beliefs? Which beliefs were in conflict? And how unsettling where these discrepancies? Take stock of the magnitude of this potential disruption in your life.

- **Experience the dissonance.** Next, take a moment to see how this dissonance makes you feel. What emotions are you experiencing? Do you feel anger or shame or embarrassment or guilt? Or perhaps you feel freedom or joy or awe or curiosity? Many times, people have a combination of feelings when reflecting on religion and their religious past, and those feelings can change over time. As we become aware of how we're feeling toward religion, we can use that emotional information to shape our decisions. And if we are regularly checking in with our dissonance and its associated emotions, we can use that as a barometer to let us know the ways in which we've changed.

- **Comfort yourself.** It can be reassuring to realize you are not alone; many people have experienced, and are experiencing, departures from their religious traditions. And many find thriving, fulfilled, and flourishing lives after leaving religion. At times, walking away from religion feels overwhelming and hopeless, as well as scary and wrong. Other times, it feels exhilarating and awe-inspiring. And some days, you feel all of those ways before lunch. Your mind and body have to process the significant shifts you're making in your identity and beliefs. It takes time to move through this process. Try to give yourself a bit of compassion and be patient as you work through this complex change. With time, attention, and plenty of support, you will experience flourishing—perhaps sooner than you think.

A CLARIFYING PICTURE

Examining the stories offered by those who have left religion helps provide a clearer picture about the reasons people are leaving religion. We're experiencing increased secularization as people outgrow their faith for intellectual reasons, augmented by a departure from religion because of traumatic abuse and an inability to make sense of senseless suffering in a cultural moment when people want to distance themselves from a label that does not represent their values. These streams of departure converge to form a large movement away from one's faith. And like many departures, there are mixed emotions and consequences associated with saying goodbye.

CHAPTER 2

AFTER RELIGIOUS TRAUMA

Of the four horsemen driving people away from religion, religious trauma appears to be a special case, deserving of its own chapter. It's a more complicated process than some of the other reasons, and it often leaves a pain that is more enduring. It's a deeper and more complex wound that cuts across our psyche, showing up unexpectedly and affecting many different areas of our life. In fact, there needs to be more psychological care for people who have endured religious trauma.

The other reason why more attention is needed for religious trauma is because there is a wide breadth or spectrum of religious trauma that people can endure. Some have suffered abuse at the hands of religious leaders, whereas others have survived gaslighting by religious leaders or had their doubts dismissed and questions shamed. And many times, people don't fully understand the extent to which their religious trauma has affected, and continues to affect, their psychological processes. The lasting effects of religious trauma are considerable and far-reaching. For those reasons, this chapter is specifically designed for people who have experienced trauma at the hands of religious individuals or systems.

WHAT IS RELIGIOUS TRAUMA?

Religious trauma can mean many different things, but researchers have offered a helpful definition. Specifically, *religious trauma* centers on mistreating and disempowering people who are in need of support and spiritual empowerment (Johnson & VanVonderen, 2005). More simply, it occurs when people who are in vulnerable situations and seeking help are wronged or exploited in the name of or through religious means or ends. Religious trauma may be perpetrated by a religious leader or as part of an abusive religious system. Johnson and VanVonderen also suggest that there may be a set of common characteristics of abusive religious systems:

- leaders focused on power
- overt fixation with performance, including obedience
- mandatory unspoken rules
- extreme religious beliefs
- church loyalty that supersedes loyalty to God
- communal secretness or paranoia

I'd also suggest there are a few others, including having your spiritual or theological questions or doubts dismissed, being belittled for mental health concerns on the basis of a lack of faith, being told that you needed to pray some "sin" away rather than receive genuine support, being coerced into a behavior change that did not align with your identity or values, being persuaded to internalize shame, or being forced to disclose some feature of your identity that you'd rather hold private. Indeed, the range of experiences under the auspices of religious trauma is vast. If you have emerged from a religious community such as this or have been mistreated by the abuse of power by religious leaders, it is possible you've experienced significant religious trauma.

> *Religious trauma: An experience where people who are vulnerable and seeking help are harmed in the name of religion, by religious leaders, or through religious means or ends.*

A recent review of the religious and spiritual abuse and trauma literature (Ellis et al., 2022) suggested that religious trauma usually emerges when leaders have misused power, resulting in psychological and spiritual harm. Although prevalence estimates depend on the study sample, the authors concluded that in some cases, as many as one in two research participants reported some form of religious or spiritual abuse (with this number being higher in some samples in and with some religious denominations). In addition, this review highlighted several features that made people more vulnerable to religious trauma.

First, people with marginalized identities often reported religious trauma or abuse (Ellis et al., 2022). For example, members of the LGBTQ+ community who were also religious may be more likely to report religious trauma. Such individuals may experience conflicting messages from their religious communities about inclusion, their status or standing in the church, and the morality of their identity or behavior. Some may experience shame or judgment from others. Some may be castigated, excluded, or excommunicated from their religious community. For many sexual minorities, how religious individuals and communities treated them is a severe emotional wound that understandably obstructs a potential connection with the divine or transcendent. After all, who would want to relate with a God they are told by others is angry and judgmental toward them for who they are?

Second, individuals in a vulnerable state who are strongly attracted to the religious group may be at higher risk for religious trauma (Ellis et al., 2022). Many see the church as a possible source of tangible support and emotional encouragement, and they are motivated to connect with the group. Others may seek churches when they lack a sense of meaning or a clear purpose in life. Religion is a source of purpose and significance; people feel special for connecting with a group that is collectively oriented toward a higher calling and in a community that promises to foster a genuine connection with the divine. This kind of meaning meets some of our deepest psychological needs, and it can feel intoxicating to find a place where we belong and are loved. However, if people begin to have negative experiences within the church, many may not be able to leave the community or depart from the group safely if they are vulnerable. Members of the religious group may threaten consequences if they leave, and so vulnerable individuals are unable to exit, despite a general lack of safety. Similarly, they may feel especially committed to a purpose and wonder what their life may be life if they leave. They may feel stuck.

Finally, religious trauma can also occur, and recur, when religious groups and communities deny the concerns or allegations of victims. So religious trauma is more common once it has already occurred or some people have attempted to uncover and address it. Many times, religious communities support perpetrators, especially if they are in positions of leadership, and use tactics to censure, bully, manipulate, silence, or exclude victims or those who raise concerns. Whistleblowers are punished and the offenders are protected. Not only does this reinflict trauma on those who have been abused, it also constitutes a new trauma for those not directly involved because it requires misleading the larger community and covering up the offenses of the abuser. Accordingly, systems that harbor and protect traumatizers and abusers become traumatizing and abusive in their own right. And those who were victims or have championed on behalf of survivors by making allegations are forced to leave, continuing a pattern of abuse with little recourse. It can create a vicious cycle of trauma.

When Is Someone at Heightened Risk of Religious Trauma?
• When they are LGBTQ+   • When they are in a psychologically vulnerable state   • When the religious group has a history of abuse

WHAT ARE THE EFFECTS OF RELIGIOUS TRAUMA?

Religious trauma has significant effects. It can shatter your entire worldview and way that you see yourself, other people, and make sense of the world. And it is compounded when this kind of trauma co-occurs with other abuse, such as physical or sexual abuse—all done by religious people or in the name of religious causes or purposes. Finally, it is often intensified when concerns or reports of such trauma or abuse are dismissed by those in charge or covered up by religious systems.

Researchers (Johnson & VanVonderen, 2005) have identified several long-term effects survivors of religious trauma often face:

- a distorted image of God or a higher power
- a distorted sense of one's own spirituality
- trouble accepting "grace"
- difficulty forming trusting relationships
- struggle setting and maintaining healthy boundaries

Clearly, the effects of religious trauma are profound, and they affect one's spiritual and relational lives in deep and lasting ways.

More recently, research has examined the unique role of religious trauma above and beyond other forms of trauma. Indeed, because religious trauma may occur with other trauma or abuse, this work examined the unique contributions of religious trauma in psychological and spiritual functioning (Ellis et al., in press). Notably, in a sample of more than 300 adults, religious trauma uniquely predicted greater religious and spiritual struggles, depression, anxiety, and trauma-related symptoms, even when accounting for the frequency of other traumatic experiences in their life. This suggests that religious trauma is, indeed, a unique and powerful form of trauma associated with people experiencing religious and spiritual struggles (e.g., difficulty in their religious life), mental health symptoms (e.g., anxiety and depression), and symptoms of trauma (e.g., loneliness, pain).

Taken together, the effects of religious trauma extend throughout one's life. If you've survived religious trauma and abuse, you may have noted this as well. Your religious and spiritual life may range from strained to shattered to nonexistent. Your view of spirituality, especially your own, has changed drastically. You may experience anxiety and depression. You may have trouble in your relationships, both in setting and holding boundaries, as well as trusting other people. And any concept of "grace" or other religiously loaded terms may feel hollow and manipulative. Spiritually and socially, religious trauma can wreak havoc.

THE CASCADING EROSION OF TRUST

I tend to think of the consequences of religious trauma as the cascading erosion of trust. First, and perhaps most devastatingly, you may lose your ability to trust yourself. Because the whole way you viewed the world was shattered, and when you spoke up and shared concerns, you were silenced, dismissed, or blamed outright, you may have learned to stop listening to yourself. You may have developed a persistent doubt in your own perception, discounting your feelings and perspective of the world. Because the perpetrators of the trauma sought to maintain power and control, you may have been told that you were "crazy" or "making things up," or perhaps you were told that you simply needed to be more spiritual. Feelings of blame, fear, and distrust are common because religious and spiritual abuse and trauma are often experienced as an assault on one's core sense of self (Oakley, 2009). In short, you were told, repeatedly, that your view of reality was wrong and you had to adopt their way of seeing the world. Ignoring your instincts became second nature, and now you don't feel you can trust you own view of the world or others. You may have internalized other people's deceit and are now unable to trust you own feelings or perceptions.

Second, you may lose trust in other people. Given that you were unjustly manipulated and unfairly exploited, you may wonder if everyone is out to get you. Understandably, a defensive response of self-protection and avoidance is often adaptive. You may avoid intimacy and become increasingly self-reliant and private. Fearing future hurt, you may avoid being vulnerable. In many ways, religious abuse and trauma may impede people's ability to form trusting relationships (Johnson & VanVonderen, 2005). Alternatively, for some, you may have difficulty knowing whom to trust, so you may seek out other people to make those decisions for you, knowing that your ability to assess the trustworthiness of others may be inaccurate. Accordingly, depending on whom you rely to help determine the trustworthiness of others, you may be susceptible to further manipulation. Over time, you may view others cynically, doubting that there are kind and good-hearted people who are not duplicitous or secretly maneuvering for their own personal gain.

Third, you may lose trust in institutions or larger systems. Rightfully, you may become suspicious of large collectives who ask you to put your faith in them and sacrifice for the greater good, including churches (Oakley & Kinmond, 2014). After all, you may have witnessed firsthand how organizations may cover up controversies, silence victims, and side with offenders, all in the name of preserving an image or brand. This unleashes new trauma and betrays a sense of deceit that can make you wary to believe any collection of people working together truly has your best interest in mind. You may expect future organizations or institutions to operate out of a similar self-interest. And you may want nothing to do with organized religion or collective group efforts again.

Finally, you may even lose trust in God (or a higher power). Because of the manipulation of religious leaders and the actions of those who have perpetrated trauma, your view of God may have been deeply altered or warped. One study reported that nearly 15% of survivors report distrust in God after religious abuse and trauma (Oakley & Kinmond, 2014). You may wonder how a supposedly kind or loving being would allow this kind of reprehensible behavior to be done in their name. Or you may question whether any religion is even worthwhile or honest, or if people were merely hiding behind a religious label to perpetrate harms and exploit others. Religion, as a whole, and perhaps any intimation of the sacred or divine may have been forever tainted by the horrific actions of abusers.

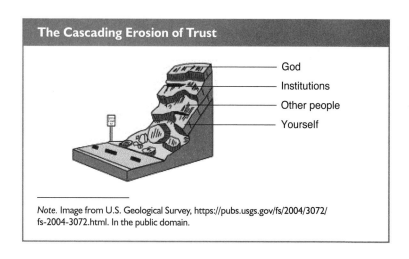

The Cascading Erosion of Trust

God
Institutions
Other people
Yourself

Note. Image from U.S. Geological Survey, https://pubs.usgs.gov/fs/2004/3072/fs-2004-3072.html. In the public domain.

The cascading erosion of trust is significant and requires help to heal. A full discussion of this process is well beyond the scope of this book, but I see two promising initial steps toward processing your trauma. First, I strongly recommend that you connect with a trained mental health therapist who has specialization in or experience working with clients who have experienced religious abuse and trauma. A deep knowledge of religion and spiritual processes is important. Some clinicians do not fully understand the nuances or complexities of religious trauma, nor can they appreciate the lingering effects of one's religious history; sometimes symptoms of religious trauma are missed or go undiagnosed. Seeking out a qualified and experienced therapist is critical for your support in processing your experiences. Second, finding a supportive and loving community is incredibly valuable. Being able to surround yourself with people who accept you for who you are and treat you with respect and care can go a long way toward rebuilding trust with others. It is worth the time and energy to identify and invest in such a supportive group.

BEWARE OF SPIRITUAL NARCISSISM

Systems that enable religious trauma and abuse can perpetuate spiritual narcissism. All of us tend to have a drive toward self-enhancement, or viewing ourselves overly positively, especially in relation to others (Gebauer et al., 2013). This tendency also shows up in religious beliefs and expressions (Gebauer et al., 2017). Although we all self-enhance some, there are individual differences, and some people are more prone to view themselves as grandiose or superior, both because of their religious views and in the domains of their religion. Here, I use the term *spiritual narcissism* to refer to those who use religion to justify their perceived self-superiority. Because religious trauma is the misuse of power by religious leaders that results in the mistreatment of the people they are leading, many times these abusive leaders rely on unquestionable spiritual authority to justify their actions. This spiritual narcissism is insidious, in part because it relies on a set of internally reinforcing rules that defies logic:

1. A leader is appointed by God;
2. leaders have special insight into and communication with God;
3. leaders can justify their actions as God's will;
4. followers are to obey and submit to a leader's authority, as God's agent, so;
5. leaders' actions are Godly and right, and followers need to submit in all circumstances.

In the end, nearly anything a leader does can be attributed to God's will or is seen as being blessed by God's will or favor. And to question or push against it is a direct violation of a follower's mandate for submissive obedience: Leaders are right by spiritual default.

I attended a Christian college, where several men developed the reputation as spiritual leaders. Conveniently, these leaders would break up with romantic partners by offering a reason that "God had told them to end their relationship" or "because they were seeking God and didn't want this relationship to get in the way." In reality, they lacked the courage to take ownership and responsibility for their choices and hid behind an impenetrable defense of spirituality. Not only could they get their way, they looked especially pious doing so. And imagine everyone's surprise when they found a new romantic partner shortly after. I suppose God does "work in mysterious ways."

More seriously and nefariously, religious leaders at churches or major communities often justify their actions and imbue them with religious rationalization because they are spiritual narcissists. They believe they have a special connection with God that others do not, and so they arrogantly rely on their own interpretation of the world and religious texts, excluding other viewpoints while being unwilling to listen to other perspectives. After all, who can argue with you if you say God told you to do something? It's a form of defensive religiousness that is often associated with prejudice and aggression, and, if unchecked, is a recipe for religious trauma and abuse (see Beck, 2004, 2006). When religious systems encourage and support spiritually narcissistic leaders, they are creating structures where trauma recurs and abusers are silenced and discredited. It can be dangerous and catastrophic.

I suspect we're especially likely to see spiritual narcissism develop among religious leaders who are viewed as heroes and lack accountability and the presence of truth-tellers in their lives. In fact, some spiritual narcissists are drawn to positions of religious leadership for the very reason that they can claim ultimate spiritual authority and wield considerable power while being adored within structures designed to support rather than challenge them. They are the central icon or representation for the whole community, and they are esteemed as untouchable and nearly perfect. As their moral status gains illusory heights, the mere action of them behaving in a certain way makes such actions right—it's like a moral self-fulfilling prophecy. If the hero-pastor does it, it must be fine. Who am I to question? But as history has taught us, power corrupts, and absolute power corrupts absolutely.

TOWARD WHOLENESS

If you've experienced religious trauma or abuse, I feel deep sympathy and compassion for you. You have been unfairly and unjustly treated. You have endured significant pain and suffering and are still living with the ramifications of the actions of others. I don't have an easy fix or quick solution for your deep grief or sorrow. For many people who have survived religious trauma, leaving church

To Cope With Religious Trauma

- Name the trauma.
- Seek therapy.
- Seek a supportive community.
- Consider reporting the abuse.
- Consider leaving your abusive religion.
- Childhelp National Child Abuse Hotline: 800-422-4453
- National Sexual Assault Hotline: 800-656-4673

and walking away from religion (at least for a time) may be the single best thing they can do to seek a life of recovery and flourishing. You are not captive to your abusers or the abusive system. Walking away is one step in the authentic journey of healing and wholeness.

And for many, as I have said already, leaving religion is just the first step in a longer process that also includes therapy. Still, another important step toward wholeness is to honestly name the trauma for what it was and take action steps toward justice. For those who have been victims of physical or sexual abuse committed by religious leaders, notifying officials or making a police report can often be a step toward justice and helping stop the cycle of abuse against others. Many people are rightfully fearful to take this course of action, fearing retribution from church leaders or congregants. Some worry about losing their social community or the potential consequences of coming forward with allegations. Again, these are thorny issues best navigated with the support of a trained professional, but there are many resources available, including reporting to the Childhelp National Child Abuse Hotline (1-800-422-4453) or the National Sexual Assault Hotline (1-800-656-4673). Part of the process of moving forward after religious trauma is regaining a sense of agency, and for some, actions such as this help in that restoration process.

Finding a qualified therapist is critical, but the process can feel daunting. Qualified therapists have graduate degrees (e.g., MSW, MA, PhD, PsyD) from accredited universities and are licensed in their state (e.g., LCSW, LPC). Therapists equipped to help offer support in the wake of religious and spiritual abuse and trauma are comfortable with, and have experience with, discussing religious and spiritual issues and concerns. Many have additional training in trauma-related practices. Some may even advertise in their biography that they have experience with religious and spiritual trauma and abuse. Online resources, such as *Psychology Today* or *Therapist.com*, host a list of therapists that can be searched by area of expertise and location. It may take some time to find a therapist that understands your background, but by allowing yourself to prioritize your care and find a good fit, you will be able to then find the support you need.

Finding a supportive community is likewise important but can seem overwhelming. Especially for those who have made many social connections through religious communities, such as church, it can be difficult to know where to start. Beginning with the safe relationships we already have and slowly sharing some of our story is a good start. It's important to set healthy boundaries here, especially if religious and spiritual trauma has made trust difficult. Some may want to disclose the full depths of their pain and abuse all at once, whereas others may never want to share anything at all. It is entirely up to you when, and how much (if anything), to share with others. But finding a group that cares to know you, and where you can feel supported and accepted for authentically sharing parts of your history can help the healing process. In many cases, people who have also experienced some religious pain, or who aren't particularly religious, might be more open to hearing what you care to share than those who are still strongly involved in their religious communities. Sometimes, starting small and slowly is a good way to share some of your history. You can frame it as being motivated to let them know more about your past and what has informed who you are as you are getting to know each other. And this can be balanced by ensuring that your social group also does plenty of other things completely unrelated to religion—things that build community, fun, and connection. Often, the practical presence of other people who care for us just as we are, without expectation of a certain set of behaviors in response, can be transformational and healing.

My hope is that you will find a way toward wholeness and healing. Religious trauma and abuse are sadly becoming common bylines of church life. It should not be this way. As you navigate the process of leaving religion, my hope is that you will find a new identity, centered on authenticity, where you can flourish. This process will take time; in fact, it may take longer than you imagine. As we'll soon see, the effects of religion continue to linger well after we walk away.

CHAPTER 3

WALKING AWAY FROM RELIGION

What does it mean to walk away from religion? Religion is deeply personal, and it's likely that it means slightly different things to different people. But there are also some commonalities in how people experience, and depart from, religion. In this chapter, we'll examine the process of religious deconstruction and how it sometimes leads to revision and reconstructing one's religious beliefs, and other times leads to leaving religion altogether. We'll also explore different ways someone's religious experience might change as a result of this deconstruction process. To begin, we'll take a closer look at where people might be starting from.

WHERE ARE PEOPLE STARTING FROM?

Everyone has a different religious experience. And people are starting from many different places when they decide to walk away from religion. Depending on your religious background and the kind of religious experience you're leaving, walking away may be harder or easier, may accompany a different set of emotional or social consequences, and may be a shorter or longer process. It may also be more costly—emotionally and socially. Some people risk nearly everything to leave religion, and others may walk away after some part of their life has been shattered. Understanding that not everyone is starting from the same place, let's briefly look at some common points of departure from religion.

Some people are leaving a casual religious identity. For example, some people may have been raised religious, but religion did not occupy a central part of their identity or take up much of their social or emotional life. They may have been religious in name only, occasionally attending religious services or engaging in religious activities, but it was not a primary way that they viewed themselves or the world around them. Likely, leaving religion may not entail as large of a shift in their life, given its already minimal importance.

For some who are leaving, religion has occupied a more central role in their lives. Many are leaving more conservative or fundamentalist upbringings, wherein nearly every aspect of their life was saturated with religion and viewed through a particular lens. In such cases, religious communities were a primary source of social ties and friends, and people made significant behavioral choices to align with their beliefs, including decisions around sex (e.g., purity culture), their body (e.g., piercings, tattoos, permissible foods), education (e.g., which college or university to attend), romantic partners (e.g., who they were allowed to date or pursue romantically), gender roles (e.g., how to navigate relationships), and career (e.g., what college major or jobs to pursue). Religious teachings likely made clear the behaviors one should be doing and the ones to avoid, and many people arranged their life accordingly. In addition, a particular set of beliefs was likely offered as absolute truth, and alternatives were spiritually corrupt or intentionally misleading. The "outside culture" was dangerous and in need of saving through conversion and adherence to religious dogma. Teachings may have centered on fear, and authority and certainty were highly lauded virtues. If you are departing, or have departed, from this background, you likely have a considerably longer process of religious change, and the lingering effects of your upbringing are probably significantly greater than those for whom religion was not as important or pervasive. Still others are leaving cults or isolated religious communities. Although many of the characteristics of these communities mirror the aforementioned dimensions of conservative fundamentalism, there is likely more at stake. Some people may risk social connections, financial resources, or even their safety to leave certain religious groups. In some situations, leaving religion means walking away from family, friends, work, financial possibilities, and one's whole life. It can require starting over. Accordingly, such a decision is weighty, and the consequences are significant.

Many people leaving religion have experienced deep pain at the hand of religious leaders or organizations. The persistent pain from these offenses will alter how people think and feel about religion, religious people, and religious organizations. Walking away may feel simultaneously freeing and frightening. Each of our religious histories is unique. However, there are some themes that folks many encounter in their process of walking away.

RELIGIOUS DECONSTRUCTION

Leaving religion typically starts with religious deconstruction. Religious deconstruction is the process by which people (a) experience doubt about their religious beliefs, practices, or identity, leading them to (b) examine and question their existing faith structures in light of new evidence or experiences, which is often accompanied by (c) a period of struggle, anxiety, and potential isolation, and which leads to (d) a revised religious experience and identity. This may or may not lead people away from religion—some leave, but others revise their religious beliefs but are still decidedly religious. In this process of doubt, questioning, struggle, and revision, I'll use myself as an example to unpack each of these.

Religious Deconstruction

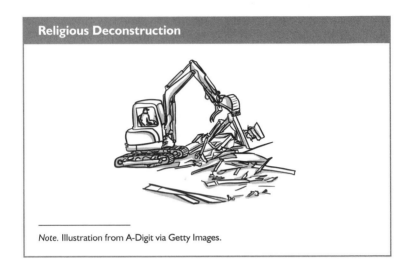

Note. Illustration from A-Digit via Getty Images.

Doubt

First, when undergoing religious deconstruction, it's quite common to experience *doubt* or a loss of certainty around beliefs. This is often triggered by a life event in which there is a discrepancy between your existing beliefs and your experience in the world. When I was 28 years old and in my fourth year of my doctoral program, my brother tragically and unexpected passed away. He was having a heart surgery that, although it carried risk, was supposed to result in repairing his heart and improving his quality of life. Heartbreakingly, the surgery was more complicated than expected, and he did not respond well. He passed away, leaving behind his wife and three children under age 6.

I was raised in a conservative evangelical Christian home. I was baptized as an infant and brought up attending church once or twice per week. And outside of my first year as a college student, I was educated in religious schools from preschool through college. My graduate training was at state schools, but I was formatively influenced by religious teaching, which prioritized God's love and justice, mercy and wrath, heaven and hell. To be sure, I believed that good things happened to those whom I love and who love God—which described my brother—and it was incomprehensible to me that he could be taken so young. How could a loving and just God allow my brother to die at 34, my sister-in-law to be widowed at 33, and their three kids to be without a father before entering elementary school? It felt absurd or evil, and I spent the next decade sorting out which of the two it was.

Although I'm a curious person who enjoys asking questions and had wrestled with my faith at various points throughout my life—most notably during college—this was decidedly different. The loss of my brother plunged me deep into doubt and was the first step in the long journey of religious deconstruction. What previously were whispers of uncertainty suddenly roared loudly with deafening doubt. I doubted whether God was good, or even existed. I doubted whether I could trust anything I was taught. I doubted whether my central organizing framework for making sense of the world was valid. My view of God and assumptions about the world no longer fit. It felt like everything I learned was a lie. So, in turn, I began to question everything.

Questioning

Doubt in one area spilled over into doubt in nearly every area, leading to *questioning*. Sometimes people are able to dismiss their doubts: They redouble their commitments or brush off their doubts by reminding themselves of their faith. However, when the doubt is simply too great or the violation is too severe, doubt gives way to questioning. Here, rather than pull back from doubt, it is viewed as an invitation to fully probe and thoroughly examine each specific belief I held. In this second phase, I interrogated all my beliefs. I chased those doubts to see where they would lead. At a basic level, was God good? Or was there even a God at all? Or had I just convinced myself to believe in God because I was raised in a religious household that made religious belief ordinary and expected, so I had just been spending most of my life assimilating my experiences into a preexisting cognitive framework that propped up a mandatory belief in God? And if there was no God, what does that mean for nearly every decision I had previously made that had even the slightest spiritual implications: where I went to college (a religious undergraduate institution), my profession (or calling), whom I married, who my friends were, and what I thought was important in life. Pulling on this "god thread" seemed to unravel the entire fabric of my worldview.

Questions were more pervasive than answers. And for a while, this was fine. Many of us enjoy thinking and spend time wrestling with cognitively challenging questions or complicated conundrums. But it's quite different when you're sorting through your own existential baggage—especially when you've internalized that such questioning might have eternal consequences in the midst of suffering and grieving. Who wants to get a question wrong if it means spending eternity in everlasting conscious torment?

The other problem that can arise is that persistent questioning can be stressful and exhausting. The brain is a problem-solving and meaning-making organ. It operates to make sense of the world and interpret it in meaningful ways, so we can navigate it effectively. A lack of answers and perpetual uncertainty can be draining. The longer we go without a structure or framework by which we can make sense of the world, the more stressed and exhausted we get. And this has effects on our mental health. I was depressed and angry. I felt foolish and bitter. I embraced cynicism as the only reasonable perspective, shrugging off life as a cruel joke where we humans were the punchline. I started to languish. Nihilism was my only comfort in a world so cold and unkind.

Struggles

Over time, persistent questioning can give way to *struggles*, characterized by groundlessness, uncertainty, anxiety, and depression.

I was wretched thinking that my changing religious beliefs might land me in hell. After all, that's partly what I was taught growing up. I was also exhausted after having examined all my beliefs. Without a solid meaning structure or worldview, life felt like an absurd joke, and I slid into a nihilistic depression. Existential malaise permeated my life. I asked myself what the point was, given that everything I had been taught felt like a complete fabrication. I was struggling with coming to terms with my new reality. I felt pretty miserable.

I constantly tried to assess what was true and what was fiction. How could I be sure what to believe? I was disoriented and angry. I was angry that a belief structure that I spent so much of my life constructing, endorsing, defending, and praising was now nothing more than rubble. I was angry that my brother was gone. I was angry that this was my life. And I was angry at all the people who could go on believing and seemed perfectly happy and contented. I was pretty unbearable to be around.

These struggles can take different shapes. Expert Julie Exline talks about six kinds of religious and spiritual struggles that people often face (Exline et al., 2014). Sometimes people have divine struggles, such as when they feel angry at God, feel God is testing them, or perceive that they are under attack from demonic or malevolent forces. In these cases, their struggles are unseen, with God or the devil. Other times, struggles are interpersonal, such as when they have disagreements with religious people or institutions. This can look like arguments with religious folks or feeling ostracized or abandoned by the church. And still other struggles are intrapersonal, centering around moral decisions, doubting, or ultimate meaning. This can look like wrestling with doubt or questioning the meaning of life. These struggles can give way to poorer psychological adjustment and mental health (Bockrath et al., 2022). And notably, sometimes these struggles are related to leaving religion. In fact, struggles may be the final straw that precedes leaving religion (Exline et al., 2022).

Revision

Over time, I figured I had to step out of this existential dread. I spent more than a few years there, but nihilism is like a layover—it's a fine place to stop, but few people want to stay there forever. Without meaning, we languish. And I was languishing. So I started reevaluating potential beliefs in light of evidence as I constructed a new identity and worldview. I wasn't sure where I'd end up, but I knew I couldn't stay in a state of disarray forever. So I started the long, slow slog of rebuilding, brick by brick, some form of a worldview. I made a few commitments. First, I valued evidence. I wasn't going to discount anything I personally experienced for the sake of a rigid belief or other people's viewpoints. I knew what I went through, and that had to fit into my worldview. Second, I tried to embrace humility. I admitted that I didn't have to have everything figured out. I acknowledged how little I actually know and how freeing that was to confess. I made friends with uncertainty. Third, I allowed myself to test different perspectives. I evaluated ideas and ideologies as they were and how they fit with my experiences. Over time, I found a new identity and a revised worldview.

This process took a long time. Years. In fact, I'd say it's still an ongoing process—and it probably always will be. I doubt I'll ever be totally settled in my religious beliefs and identity. They will probably grow and change as I do. It took me more than a decade of intentional work before I felt more stabilized. Some people can move through faster, and others take longer. I'm by no means the standard—but realize that honest and lasting religious change doesn't often happen in an instant. There are no shortcuts. Bypassing your way around the pain, grief, and anger will leave you unsatisfied and unchanged. Lasting change takes time to process. You can't rush it.

The revision process is an inflection point—it's the critical point in the religious deconstruction process where people decide whether to modify some aspects of their religion while keeping other aspects the same (reconstruction) or leave religion entirely (deidentification).

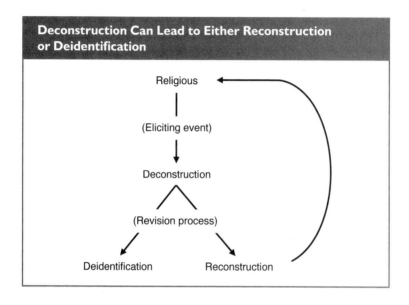

Deconstruction Can Lead to Either Reconstruction or Deidentification

Religious

(Eliciting event)

Deconstruction

(Revision process)

Deidentification   Reconstruction

After deconstruction, some people reconstruct it in ways in which they still remain religious. Of course, they are changed, and their views are altered in significant ways, but they would still identify as religious. However, for others, deconstructing their faith leads them to leave their religion behind. Their revision lands them outside of the traditional confines of religion, in a new territory. A primary question is whether one continues to consider themselves to be religious after revising their beliefs. Some do, and their process of reconstruction means they remain religious. For others who decide to leave religion, they enter into a process of religious deidentification.

RELIGIOUS DEIDENTIFICATION

Religious deidentification is the process by which people no longer identify as religious. Previous scholars have suggested four or five components of the process: losing religious experiences, intellectual denial, emotional suffering, moral criticism, and leaving one's religious community (Barbour, 1994; Streib, 2021). These can be thought of as the cognitive, emotional, moral, and social components of leaving religion.

Leaving religion may look different for each individual. One of my relatives has been a consistent deacon at his church for several decades but has never believed in God; he loves the social aspect of religion but cannot intellectually assent to any religious notion of the supernatural. He wouldn't consider himself religious because he does not believe in God. Conversely, a friend of mine has cultivated a deep relationship with God but stopped going to church several years ago. She considers her faith to be private and does not want the label of being "religious" nor does she want to associate with other religious individuals. So when people stop identifying as religious, it does not mean all features of religion cease; rather, a departure may involve some features (Van Tongeren & DeWall, 2023). Moreover, it may be a process, where certain features erode more quickly (or slowly) than others (Saroglou, 2011). We'll examine each component in turn.

Multiple Ways to Leave Religion

- Disbelieve in God or the tenets of one's faith: "I no longer believe that the stories in the Bible are true."
- Emotionally disengage from God: "I no longer pray because I don't feel close to God."
- Discontinue adhering to the behavioral requirements of one's religion: "I no longer follow my religion's prohibition against sex before marriage."
- Disaffiliating from one's religious community: "I no longer attend church-related social events."

Disbelief in God or Other Religious Tenets

The cognitive feature of deidentification involves no longer believing in God or in specific tenets of one's religion. Other researchers call this intellectual denial. It is possible that religious doubt may give way to disbelief. For example, a devout Christian may stop believing that God exists after questioning how a good and loving supernatural being could allow tragedy to afflict their loved ones. Recall that more than half of one sample of religious dones reported intellectual reasons for leaving their faith (McLaughlin et al., 2022). This likely resulted in them no longer believing in God.

Although there are good reasons to conclude that disbelief must be a primary feature of deidentification—and anyone who disbelieves would immediately cease all other forms of religious behavior—I'm not convinced this is the case. Not only does my relative's steadfast commitment to serving in church despite his disbelief in God give me pause, but so, too, does a conversation I had with a pastor at the ex-evangelical conference I attended on changing faith. In a small group session, I started chatting with a senior pastor of a small church who confided in me that he started seriously questioning his faith nearly a decade ago. Then, after several years of wrestling, he concluded that God was not real, and he effectively became an atheist. However, he didn't quit his job. He was in his 50s, and knowing that retirement was on the horizon, he didn't want to jeopardize his financial future by leaving his career and seeking new employment so late in life. Instead, he kept his disbelief private and continued serving as a pastor, facilitating other people's connection with God. He admitted that other than his wife, no one else knew of his inner conflict.

One other point deserves mentioning. Many of us may wander back and forth between belief and disbelief without a public declaration of our lack of belief. Although some indeed proclaim they do not believe, for many, this disbelief is a quieter, more personal matter. Depending on our particular religious upbringing, it may also be one that we're not ready to admit to ourselves, even when we're fairly sure we no longer believe.

Emotional Disengagement From God

The emotional component of deidentification involves no longer trying to relationally engage with the sacred or divine. This looks a lot like stopping any of the behaviors or rituals designed to foster connection with God, such as prayer, singing, worship, reading holy texts, meditating, or participating in religious ceremonies. Some previous scholars have called this the emotional suffering phase of deconversion. This disengagement may be brought on by experiencing spiritual struggles with God. Indeed, in a large sample of college students, such struggles were associated with pulling away from religion (Exline et al., 2022).

Importantly, experiencing a lack of closeness to, or even anger toward, God or the sacred is not disengagement. Plenty of religious people experience periods of "spiritual dryness," wherein they do not feel close to God, despite their best efforts (Wang, 2011). Indeed, many religious individuals experience seasons when they either feel distant from or deserted by God, yet they continue to pursue a relational connection with the divine. And for some, this may lead to a deepening of their faith and spiritual maturation. Conversely, disengagement is intentionally or consciously ceasing those actions designed to nurture spiritual closeness with the sacred. People may disengage because they feel angry at, bitter toward, or harbor resentment or contempt toward God. They may not want anything to do with sacred connection. What differentiates disengagement from dryness or (perceived) desertion is the primary party responsible for the relational distance: The person is volitionally walking away rather than still seeking connection despite a lack of feeling close to God or the divine.

In college, I experienced a period of spiritual dryness. I really was trying to have a deeper, more emotionally rich connection with God, but it felt elusive. For more than a year, I tried everything to rekindle the relationship with God that I once had but came up wanting. I felt as if I were calling God, hoping for communion, only to have no one answer. I was willing, but God felt absent. In contrast, when my brother died, I was the one who stopped calling. I needed space, and interacting with a God who would allow, or cause, such tragedy to befall my brother seemed incomprehensible. I didn't want a relationship with a god like that. I disengaged completely.

Discontinuance of Adherence to Behavioral Mandates

The moral or behavioral component of deidentification is when people stop following the moral rules or mandates of a religion. Some researchers call this moral criticism. Religion has a lot to say about how people should live. Such teachings and messages often center around things to do (prescriptions), such as being forgiving, loving, and generous, as well as things not to do (proscriptions), such as imposing regulations around the body, including guidelines around food and sex. Likely, when people discontinue adhering to the moral teachings of their religion, they'll likely stop following the proscriptions—things religion has long taught them they should not do. Whereas some may cease being as patient or forgiving, research suggests those prosocial parts of religion tend to linger (Van Tongeren, DeWall, Chen, et al., 2021). And while we'll unpack that process more a little later in the book, the point here is that most often, people pull away from religious teaching around morality precisely because they no longer agree with the moral restrictions of their religion.

Religion has a long history of telling people how to manage their body: the food they should and shouldn't eat, what sexuality should look like, and what substances they can or cannot consume.

It often offers a set of restrictions to maintain a sense of "purity" for the body. Indeed, many religious teachings see the body as a temple or dwelling place of a spirit, so it's the person's job to make sure this house is up to the spiritual standards of hosting a divine presence. When people stop adhering to the moral mandates of religion, they often loosen these restrictions. They broaden and explore outside previous boundaries. They eat what they please, change their view of healthy sexuality, or consume substances previously forbidden. Their morals and values change, and their behavior follows. This is not to say there is not another framework or standard that guides their behavior, but rather, such guidance is no longer based primarily on their religious teachings.

Disaffiliating From One's Religious Community

The social component of deidentification involves distancing and disconnecting from one's religious community. When people disconnect from their community, they stop attending religious gatherings and largely distance themselves from religious institutions. This doesn't mean they cut out any friend or social bond with religious ties; rather, their participation in formal religious gatherings or connections to official religious institutions is severed. They stop going to church or mosque or attending temple, or they give up on their small group or Bible study. While they may continue to maintain friendships or familial relationships with religious individuals, their public connection to a religious community ceases.

Although disconnection from community is particularly public, leaving a religious community doesn't mean that people have necessarily abandoned all their religious practices or given up on their spiritual connection with something larger than themselves. Plenty of people find spiritual connection, and perhaps a deeper connection, outside of traditional religious settings. Some are so frustrated, hurt, discouraged, or disgusted with religious institutions that they cannot in good conscience attend their gatherings or publicly avow to being part of their community. Others have simply not found a place of worship that aligns with their values, beliefs, and practices and so have endeavored to seek a divine relationship outside of a formal social group. The 2020 pandemic largely disrupted religious gatherings and stalled social connection. For many, it also served as a catalyst to stop attending church regularly; after having found they could get along just fine without their religious community, many never returned after restrictions were lifted and their gatherings reconvened.

DISTINCT DEPARTURES

What the previous sections reveal is that there is no singular or "right" way to leave religion. Each person's process of deidentification looks unique. For example, someone who stopped attending church but privately believes and seeks an emotional connection with the sacred while no longer adhering to religion's strict moral mandates is quite different from someone who attends a mosque and follows the moral rules of their religion but privately disbelieves, feeling no emotional connection to the divine. And once you treat deidentification from these four features of religion as a matter of degree, you quickly realize how many distinct departures from religion there actually are. Each person's narrative and experience are different.

Even though each departure looks different, my colleagues and I have done some cross-cultural research investigating broader categories of folks making this transition away from religion. We found two larger groups of religious dones (i.e., people who left religion): those who truly left and those who were still likely actively engaged in religious practices (McLaughlin et al., 2022). The *discontinued dones*, who truly left religion, were those who were less likely to believe in God, were less committed to their beliefs, much less likely to engage in religious practices or associate with religious individuals, and much more likely to hold less positive views toward religious people or religion in general. In short, they were completely done with religion. On the other hand, the *still-practicing dones*, who were still actively engaged in religious practices despite no longer considering themselves "religious," were those who were more likely to still believe in God and hold such beliefs with greater commitment and to continue practicing aspects of their religion and associating with religious individuals; they also held more positive attitudes toward other religious people and religion in general. Despite deidentifying from religion, their behavior was still rather religious. This continued practice took an emotional toll. Compared with discontinued dones, still-practicing dones reported less positive and more negative affect/emotions, greater anxiety, and greater depression.

The way the study was set up precludes firm causal conclusions, but the data are suggestive. It might be that the dissonance associated with deidentifying but still practicing exacts a psychological premium. Of course, it could also be that poorer mental health is leading dones to remain engaged in their religious communities, or perhaps something else is causing both deidentification and worsened emotional experiences. But regardless of the cause, still practicing dones report poorer mental health. And this suggests deidentification without altering religious behavior may not be a tenable long-term solution. So if departures look different, where, exactly, do people end up at the end of this process? That is, where do they land?

WHAT DOES RELIGIOUS CHANGE LOOK LIKE?

Religious change may show up in various ways after people walk away. Some people undergo (a) *de-emphasis*, others harbor (b) *antipathy*, and still others find (c) *secular spirituality*. Of course, this list is not exhaustive, and some people experience multiple changes, but

Different Changes After Leaving Religion

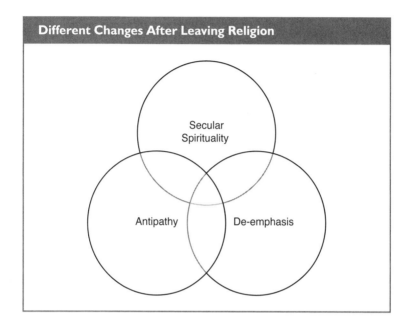

Secular Spirituality

Antipathy

De-emphasis

we'll take a look at each of these shifts in one's life as a result of religious change.

De-emphasis is when people deprioritize the role religion plays in their life. Walking away from religion may result in other aspects of their life assuming greater prominence. Perhaps some focus on their career, invest in relationships, or intensify interest in a hobby. For those who de-emphasize, their attitudes toward religion may be relatively benign or indifferent. They may not hold particularly strong or negative attitudes; perhaps they may even be grateful for the role of religion earlier in their lives but no longer feel as though it fits. Like a flame on a melting candle that has extinguished, religion has simply run its course and no longer has the same value or impact. Many who de-emphasize religion don't necessarily harbor negative feelings toward religion.

For example, recall that nearly half of the participants in a study on religious deidentification reported outgrowing religion (or intellectual motivations) as the primary reason for leaving religion (McLaughlin et al., 2022). Among these, many simply found new ways of making sense of the world. Perhaps formal education or a particular career provided a new lens through which they understand themselves and others. As a new mental framework for interacting with the world became more valuable, religion's utility faded away. It merely lost prominence in someone's life.

The second kind of change seems starkly different. *Antipathy* is when people hold particularly strong and negative emotions toward religion, religious people, or religious institutions. For these individuals, religion is likely still an important character in the story of their life—however, it has become a villain rather than a hero. Far from feeling neutral, they may feel anger, disgust, and mistrust toward religion or religious people. People who harbor antipathy toward religion may speak vocally against religion, highlighting its negative effect in their life, and passionately argue that others see it as ruinous and misleading. They may feel stuck in a pattern of angry rumination about their religious experiences and may commiserate with others who have left religion and similarly feel angry for their religious experiences.

For those who left religion after experiencing religious trauma or because of personal suffering, antipathy toward religion may be common. It makes sense that a source of deep pain and hurt would evoke a strong, negative emotional reaction. In fact, such a process may be rather healthy. Anger is an emotion which conveys to us that a boundary has been violated, and it alerts us to act assertively to protect ourselves (or those we love). Feeling angry after surviving religious abuse, being traumatized by religious individuals or institutions, or trying to make sense of shattered assumptions following loss or tragedy is a natural development in metabolizing suffering. It helps people create space and distance from the source of their pain and allows them to establish new boundaries where they can be safe and work toward healing. Feeling antipathy isn't bad or wrong any more than religion losing centrality is good and right; they are simply different destinations that serve different purposes depending on people's experiences with religion and reasons for leaving.

The third kind of change is when people seek *secular spirituality*. Some may find the religious structures or traditions of religion too restrictive but still desire a transcendent connection with something larger than themselves. Or perhaps some have felt hurt by religion but don't wish to disengage completely from the divine—they simply seek new avenues toward spiritual connection and meaning. When some people leave religion, they find themselves engaging with spirituality in nontraditional and largely nonreligious ways. A host of options that I might call "religion-adjacent" have become increasingly available as more people are deidentifying from religion. For example, some religious dones have become increasingly interested in the Enneagram, which has been viewed as some as a spiritual framework for understanding personality and human behavior. Others have explored nonreligious spirituality, including crystals, meditation, self-healing, breathwork, astrology, lunar synchronicity, or yoga. Still others have become students of philosophy, and others have replaced religion with therapy, personal growth, and self-discovery. In short, many seek ways to find a transcendent connection with something outside themselves and establish a deeper sense of lasting meaning. We'll return to explore this "post-religious spirituality" more thoroughly later in the book.

None of these destinations are mutually exclusive, and people may move in and out of these over their lifetime. Consider someone who is raised in a conservative religious home and experiences some mild spiritual abuse. After college, she begins to question some of the assumptions she long took for granted and experiences a shift in her beliefs. She becomes angry thinking of the different decisions that shaped her life based on religious teachings she no longer believes.

She harbors resentment toward her parents for raising her in this way and imposing their views on her when she was too young to choose her own beliefs autonomously. This strains her relationship with her parents, necessitating distance. She finds religion, as a whole, distasteful and exploitive and gets stuck in rumination about her religious past. Still wanting to connect with something larger than herself, she explores different avenues of spirituality. While working with a therapist, she processes her anger toward religion and her parents, and her anger begins to fade. She also loses some interest in her new spiritual practices, and both religion and spirituality take a less central role in her life. She finds great joy and meaning in volunteering at her local animal shelter. As she ages, she finds new ways of engaging with the world and doesn't think often of religion.

YOU ARE HERE

If you've ever been traversing a trail and found a long-awaited map posted along the path, the first and most important feature of that map is the arrow and text that says "You are here." It helps you orient yourself along your journey so you can decide where to go next. So in the process of walking away from religion, each person likely locates themselves on a different part of the path. Put differently, if everyone who walks away from religion is a religious done, you might be curious: What kind of religious done am I?

On the basis of the research discussed in this chapter, you might gravitate toward one, or more, of the following descriptors:

- *Disbelievers* are those who no longer believe in supernatural agents (like God) or core tenets of one's religion. This might mean you do not believe in God or the supernatural realm, or perhaps you've stopped believing in the deity of Christ, the value of the Eightfold Path, or reincarnation or the afterlife. You

> **In What Ways Are You a Religious Done?**
>
> - I disbelieve in God or the tenets of my religion.
> - I have emotionally disengaged from God.
> - I no longer adhere to the behavioral mandates of my religion.
> - I am no longer connected to a religious community.
> - Some combination of the above.

have given up these beliefs and likely find natural or scientific explanations more compelling.

- *Disengagers* are those who no longer interact with or have a relationship with the sacred or transcendent. This means you don't feel any connection to a spiritual being or sense of larger transcendence. The spiritual part of your life has withered.

- *Discontinuers* are those who no longer feel bound by the moral or behavioral mandates of religion. This means you no longer view religious teachings as the final authority of morality or virtue in your life. You have found other sources of moral guidance on how to best live your life.

- *Disaffiliates* are those who have left their religious communities. This means you likely no longer regularly attend religious services or religiously organized meetings or groups (e.g., Bible studies, prayer groups). Your social connections now come from other communities.

- *Spiritual but not religious* are those who remain engaged in spiritual practices but do not identify as religious. The label of "religious" no longer fits—for any number of reasons, ranging from a distaste of religion or religious people to a desire to expand beyond the restrictive confines of religion—but you still foster a deep personal spirituality. Many aspects of spiritual views have changed, even if you remain shaped by your religious history.

Of course, this list is not meant to be exhaustive, and you may identify with multiple labels. You might also identify as a religious done, yet none of these descriptors quite captures your experience or current set of beliefs or behaviors. However, my sense is that most of you will find resonance with at least one of these groups—and by doing so, you'll realize you're not alone.

RECONSTRUCTION

As mentioned earlier, deconstruction doesn't always mean someone completely leaves religion. For some, this process gives way to a reconstruction process where people reassemble their worldview in ways that are still religious. For example, consider a Buddhist who, after the process of deconstruction, no longer finds the supernatural elements of their religion appealing but is still drawn to the practical ways that following their religion may improve their life. They disbelieve that reincarnation is real but take solace in mindful meditation and find wisdom in the goal of overcoming desire as a pathway to free oneself from suffering. They would still consider themselves a Buddhist but may vary in how they live out their religious practices.

Or consider a Christian who was raised believing in the inerrancy and infallibility of the Bible, taught that God was vengeful and jealous, long believed that hell was real, and held that their religion was the only path toward salvation. After deconstructing their beliefs, this person no longer views scripture as error-free or a final authority, believes that all persons will be redeemed to a loving God, and believes Christianity is but one of many pathways toward this salvation of all people. They adopt a universal religiousness but still identify as a Christian largely because they are most comfortable with this narrative explanation of the world; it was their "native language" and the one that makes the most sense to them.

The reconstruction process may be part of an ongoing natural faith development. Fowler (1981) described different stages of faith, whereby as people move through a typical developmental trajectory as they age, their religious and spiritual beliefs similarly evolve and change. As we mature and develop cognitively, our patterns of religious thought become increasingly complex, and we must revise, or update, our religious worldviews. Not everyone moves through every stage, and life circumstances and personal characteristics play a significant role in this continued revision process. In short, for some, the deconstruction–reconstruction cycle may be part of faith maturation or development. Put differently, it may be part of someone's spiritual evolution. And rather than leave religion, some people rearrange their beliefs and practices. Surely, reconstruction and leaving religion may have somewhat liminal or fuzzy borders. Some who reconstructed have certainly left aspects of their religion but not religion altogether. After doubting, questioning, struggling, and revising their beliefs, they find merit in religion and value in the identity of being religious.

A helpful way to move through the deconstruction–reconstruction process is to consider each of the beliefs and practices you interrogated and ask yourself three questions: (a) Do I still believe this is true? (b) Does this belief or practice still align with my values? (c) Would holding this belief or engaging in this practice feel authentic? If the answers are all yes, it is likely something that, although you might have revised, you are likely to retain. If the answer is no, these are likely aspects that are discarded. For example, after reconstruction, people may continue to read scriptures or engage in prayer, despite thinking differently about each of those; perhaps scripture is now seen as a story to convey wisdom of life's truths, and prayer is more seen as a way to change oneself rather than a petition intended to change the mind of a supernatural agent.

CHARTING YOUR COURSE

Let's consider some steps to bring this research from theory into practice. I understand this is a process—and one that doesn't move linearly. People may move in and out of deconstruction and reconstruction multiple times, and some deidentify while others don't. So I'm not assuming you are at any certain point, nor do I suppose you have conclusively resolved any particular process. Understanding those important nuances, let's look at some helpful possibilities:

- **Identify your origin.** Take some time to think about where you are, or were, starting from. How central was religion in your life? Was it a primary part of your identity? Did you regularly attend services and engage in religious behaviors? Or was it more peripheral? How big of a role did it play in shaping some of your life decisions (e.g., education, career, relationships)? When you can gain awareness about the size of religion in your life, it helps prepare you for the process that is ahead.
- **Explore your deconstruction.** Deconstruction can be a destabilizing and unsettling time, so it can help to explore where you are in this process and what beliefs are the most challenging. Are there certain beliefs you know must be addressed or changed? Are some beliefs still worth holding on to? Or is it a wholesale change? Are you still experiencing doubt or questions? Are you currently struggling? Have you started revising your beliefs? Processing these questions with friends or a therapist can be valuable.
- **Identify what stays and what goes.** Because there are multiple parts of religion you may walk away from, consider what you are leaving and what might remain. Are you leaving a community or set of moral rules while retaining a belief in and a spiritual connection with the transcendent? Or do you enjoy the community but want to unfetter yourself from the baggage of beliefs

and behaviors? When you realize that our religious experiences can be uncoupled in this way, you can gain clarity around which parts you'd like to keep and which parts need to change or be abandoned altogether.

- **Routinely check in with your feelings.** Your emotions are important indicators about what you need. They can also let us know if we've made any progress in making sense of life after religion and how far we've come. Make it a practice to check in with your feelings. Do you feel anger and antipathy toward religion, or indifference and apathy? Do you feel anxiety and fear, or freedom and excitement? Or do you feel all of those at different times, or even at once? Regularly seeing how our emotions change can let us know how we've changed and what we need in the current moment.
- **Slowly revise.** Eventually, you'll land on a new set of beliefs. They may or may not be religious or spiritual. But over time, you will craft a meaningful and coherent way of seeing the world that is aligned with your values and authentic identity. Give yourself time to build this slowly. Don't rush it. Sometimes, it takes deliberate effort to build our beliefs; other times, it happens more naturally and slowly.

A LONG JOURNEY

Walking away from religion means different things to different people, depending on the role religion has played in their life. For many, religion was so important, so central, that leaving it is a life-altering decision with cascading effects throughout their life. This means it's not a singular point, but rather a longer, involved process that unfolds over time. Don't rush yourself through the process. Allow yourself the space to experience your emotions, process your feelings, and find a new way forward.

CHAPTER 4

RELIGIOUS RESIDUE

Why is it so hard to leave religion once you have made the decision to walk away? People often feel as though they can't shake certain parts of their former religious identity. For many, they feel stuck—like a clean break from religion is elusive or impossible. Sometimes, people question whether they've made any real change at all. Whether it's ongoing urges to pray or attend a religious service, continued thinking patterns, or internalized emotions, such as persistent guilt and shame, religion seems to stick around a lot longer than many people anticipated, or perhaps wanted. Others may even feel like they are getting drawn back into religion, furiously trying to escape the quicksand of their religious past. At times, you may want to rush right toward crafting a new identity and way of life, but there is a real psychological obstacle that makes a quick and complete deidentification from religion difficult.

Of course, any lasting personal change is difficult and requires considerable work, and religious change is no different. But as you'll see, leaving religion may be harder than some other changes people desire to make in their lives. Religion is a powerful, if not all-encompassing, worldview that resides at the center of people's identity. Especially among those for whom religion was a defining part of how they saw themselves and the world. And although people may be quick to notice barriers to leaving, such as family, friends, or even finances, fewer are aware of the powerful internal psychological processes operating outside of conscious awareness that allows religion to linger. For any identity change to be meaningful and lasting, we have to better understand the strong pull of religion and the lasting ways it can affect us. Only then can we begin to craft a life centered on authentic alignment with our values.

WHAT IS RELIGIOUS RESIDUE?

Religion is sticky. By this, I mean that religion imprints on us in indelible ways. My colleagues and I pioneered work in this area, and our study of participants reporting religious deidentification was powerfully

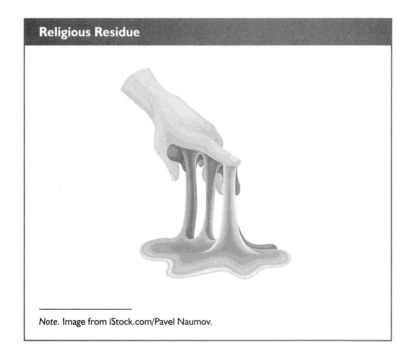

Religious Residue

Note. Image from iStock.com/Pavel Naumov.

revealing. We sampled several thousand people from various cultures around the world (Hong Kong, the Netherlands, New Zealand, the United States) and found a striking result: People who were once religious resembled currently religious people much more than those who have never been religious did (Van Tongeren, DeWall, Chen, et al., 2021). Religion leaves a residue that persists even after people deidentify. What exactly is happening and why is this the case?

Religious History Matters

When we set out to study people leaving religion, we were struck by the fact that most research (and public perception) treated the nonreligious (i.e., religious nones) as a monolithic group. This was odd to us, given that we assumed at least some of the people who did not identify as religious likely were religious at some point in their life (i.e., who we called religious dones). Because religion is a powerful social force, it seemed reasonable that having been religious in the past might exert some effect on one's current psychology and behavior. There were clues from other areas in psychology, where a significant life event can alter people's psychology moving forward. For example, research on depression found that people who had experienced a major depressive episode in their life process information differently than those who have never reported such an episode. Even though both groups may report not (or no longer) being depressed, there were significant differences in how those groups processed social information, including differences in memory, attention, implicit biases, and interpreting information about oneself (e.g., Phillips et al., 2010; Watkins & Moulds, 2007). Having been depressed in the past changes one's psychology so powerfully that there are downstream cognitive, emotional, and behavioral ramifications, even after one is no longer depressed. So, then, could being religious in the past change one's psychology as well?

87

Although the differences between being religious and being depressed are obvious (and I'm not equating the two), the lesson learned was clear: Powerful life experiences can change people in lasting ways. We wondered if religion—which is a central organizing force in many people's lives, with clear cognitive, emotional, and behavioral outcomes—may operate similarly by exerting a lingering effect after people walk away. Rather than treat all nonreligious people as the same, we made a rather straightforward, although rather novel, hypothesis: One's religious history matters.

Describing Religious Residue

My colleagues and I coined the term *religious residue* to describe how religion continues to affect people who were once religious after they have left religion. Armed with a simple but provocative hypothesis that religion leaves a residue, we started collecting data. A lot of data. And we sampled folks from around the world to make sure we weren't just explaining a purely Western or American phenomenon. The data were revealing. You're welcome to read all of the scientific details of each study[1] (in fact, I'd encourage it!), but I'll summarize the key findings here.

- **Religious attitudes persist.** Our data showed that religious dones had more positive attitudes toward God, religious people, and religion in general than those who were never religious (Van Tongeren, DeWall, Hardy, et al., 2021). In addition, religious dones tend to hold their beliefs with more certainty and

---

[1]The full details of all studies are described in DeWall and Van Tongeren (2022); Exline et al. (2022); McLaughlin et al. (2022); Schwadel et al. (2021); Van Tongeren and DeWall (2023); Van Tongeren, DeWall, Chen, et al. (2021); Van Tongeren, DeWall, Hardy, et al. (2021); Van Tongeren, DeWall, and Van Cappellen (2023).

commitment than those who were never religious, which is a holdover from their religious past. So not only what someone believes, but how they believe it, continues to be shaped by religion after people walk away.

- **Religious emotions persist.** We also found that religious emotions, such as feelings toward God, continued to persist among religious dones as well (Van Tongeren, DeWall, Chen, et al., 2021). They reported both stronger positive and negative emotions toward God than those who were never religious. This makes intuitive sense for at least two reasons. First, if some who were never religious never had any relationship with God (and may have never believed in God), they may not have strong emotions toward God at all. Second, many religious dones may also have stronger negative emotions because they are wrestling with anger toward, or feeling hurt by, God as part of leaving religion.

- **Religious behaviors persist.** Our findings revealed that people continue to have some religious engagement after deidentifying (Van Tongeren, DeWall, Chen, et al., 2021). That is, they still pray, meditate, and attend religious services more than those who were never religious. And although these were significantly less frequent than religious people, they didn't fall to the low levels of those who were never religious.

- **Prosocial behaviors persist.** Many religions teach their followers to be good, kind, and generous people (Van Tongeren, DeWall, Chen, et al., 2021). In short, religion encourages prosociality. Across separate studies, including a multiyear study, our findings show that people continue to donate their time and money significantly after leaving religion. The positive effects of religion appear to linger, too.

- **This residue persists outside of conscious awareness.** Even on a gut level, we see evidence for religious residue. When we assessed how people felt about God by using an implicit measure (asking them to reply as quickly as possible to prompts without pausing to think first), we see that religious dones show a stronger positive preference for God than those who were never religious (Van Tongeren, DeWall, Chen, et al., 2021). This means that our immediate, default reactions toward God—that happen before we can consciously think about it—may continue to be shaped by our religious histories. When it's occurring on an implicit level, you can imagine how hard it must be to shake.

- **Religious residue does fade, eventually.** We also found longitudinal evidence in a multiyear study that religious residue does fade—something we call *residual decay*. It's stronger if someone has recently left religion and weaker if someone left a longer time ago, but some residue persists (Van Tongeren, DeWall, Hardy, et al., 2021). This suggests that although it wanes over time, some religious vestiges of residue will continue to linger.
- **Ex-evangelicals may be more prone to residue.** Although there is only tentative evidence, some of our work shows that those who left Protestant Evangelicalism (i.e., ex-evangelicals) may have a harder time shaking some of the values of their upbringing (Schwadel et al., 2021). There is something about Protestant Evangelicalism that offers a potent combination of conservative religious and political values that people deeply internalize into their psychological architecture, providing it with significant staying power. Of course, more research is needed here to gain a better understanding of why this might be.

Taken together, religious residue shows up in your attitudes, emotions, and behaviors. Religious residue affects the whole person. It occurs when you're aware of it, as well as when you're not aware, operating on an unconscious level. Religious residue does get less potent over time, which means that lasting change is possible, but some residue appears to persist, suggesting it is something you may always contend with.

The Sprawling Effect of Religion

Our next step was to start exploring the different areas where we might see this residue show up. Given that religion is sticky and religious residue is pervasive, let's look at some of the areas people find religion continuing to exert an effect, even after they leave.

- **Morals.** We found that religious residue shows up in people's moral values (Van Tongeren, DeWall, Hardy, et al., 2021). Specifically, religious dones continue to endorse more conservative moral values (such as deferring to authority and maintaining purity) than those who were never religious. These are the moral values that are typically associated with religion, which indicates a clear religious residue associated with morality. As hard as it may be to hear for some religious dones, religious residue shows up in the form of the persistence of somewhat more conservative morals. However, we also found that religious dones view morality as more relativistic after leaving religion, even if the content of their moral values (i.e., endorsing more conservative values) is still shaped by their religious upbringing.
- **Values.** Here, too, we found that religious dones had more conservative personal values, defined as valuing security, conformity, and tradition, than never-religious individuals (Schwadel et al., 2021). This means that after leaving religion, religious dones may continue to desire security (e.g., living in secure surroundings, supporting the government to protect citizens from threats), endorse conformity (e.g., wanting people to do what they are told and follow the rules, behaving properly at

all times), and support tradition (e.g., remaining modest, following familial and religious customs). Even if these may be precisely some of the reasons why you left religion, you may experience a pull toward these familiar values from your religious upbringing.

- **Consumer behavior.** We also found that religious dones may be willing to spend more money on items with religious iconography or symbols, like a prayer journal or a wallet with a Bible verse, than never religious individuals (DeWall & Van Tongeren, 2022). Having spent money on things like this in the past, religious dones are likely to pay more for such items. So, we even see religious residue in where people spend their money.

Some of these findings may seem counterintuitive or may even feel threatening. After all, some of you left precisely because your religious upbringing was too conservative, or your values were overly focused on purity, security, tradition, and conformity. Why should folks who have left religion still endorse the same values that caused them to leave religion in the first place?

This speaks to the power of religious residue. Even if we consciously protest certain morals or values, the effect of our previous religious upbringing still may show up. In fact, it may just express itself differently. For example, rather than focusing on the sexual purity of your religious upbringing, perhaps you are more focused on ideological purity—ensuring that other people think and believe exactly what you do, leaving little room for difference. Or perhaps you still feel a strong pull toward conformity, but this time desiring to fit in with a new group rather than the religious group of your past. Still, these values or habits may show up in unwanted ways, when, despite our strong efforts for autonomy and freedom, we still feel ourselves seeking security and wanting a strong authority to tell us what to do. We may replace a pastor with a guru, continuing a pattern of having someone direct our life and instruct us on what and how to believe. I might even argue that it suggests religious residue is more potent and sneaky than it appears at first blush. It shows up in the most unlikely of places.

TO HELL WITH THE DEVIL

One evening over dinner, I was having a conversation with my wife about some of this research. I was sharing that a large portion of my findings on religious residue focused on "positive" things, such as pro-social behavior (like donating or volunteering), and some critics have suggested that I take a look at whether the "darker" side of religion likewise persists. My wife, Sara, is a therapist who sees, among other clients, a fair number of people who are undergoing religious change. She's an expert in helping people work through religious trauma and find meaning after religious change. And, like me, she was raised in a conservative religious home. Seeking her opinion about this work, she mentioned one area she noticed that her clients simply cannot shake is the fear of hell and the devil.

If you grew up in the church in the 1980s and 1990s (like we did), you probably learned some behaviors were strictly forbidden: taboo for any seriously religious individual. One such practice (that was a popular dare at church camps) was to go into a completely dark bathroom and recite "Bloody Mary" three times while looking into the mirror. The legend goes that doing so will evoke a malevolent spirit, which makes it quite the risky dare for religious kids at a sleepaway camp. When I asked Sara more about these persistent beliefs, she asked me whether I now (still) believed this would happen. I laughed and confirmed my disbelief. This was clearly a childish belief. So, she followed up to ask whether I would be willing to test her theory by reciting the incantation in our bathroom that evening. Without any hesitation, I firmly declined and said, "Of course I don't believe in it, but why bother tempting anything, just in case?"

I then asked whether she'd be willing to try. Naturally, she immediately and emphatically declined, offering a cheeky, "Hell, no!"

Why would both Sara and I, who have since disavowed such a legend as untrue, be so hesitant, or rather unwilling, to engage in this taboo behavior, even though we didn't believe? What is it about the darker side of religion that is so powerful that it might exert an influence even after we disbelieve?

Sara mentioned that in her work with her clients, hell and the devil continue to be areas of anxiety for religious dones. Although they no longer believe, her clients who have left religion express concern that they could be wrong—and hell, among all things, is something you simply do not want to be wrong about. This fear of eternal punishment can be a barrier to embracing one's new identity and set of beliefs. For many, the fear of the devil and an afterlife in hell was a significant source of stress as they grew up. Put simply, some people who left religion still worried that if they were wrong (and religion was correct), they'd pay the ultimate eternal price. She suggested that I collect some data and examine this empirically. So, to help provide insight on this topic, and perhaps exorcise some of my own personal demons (pun intended), I set out to run a study.

My students and I collected data from nearly 900 participants (Van Tongeren et al., in press). We focused on four different potentially "negative" features of religion. First, research has shown that religious people are more likely to see patterns where they don't exist, so we looked at illusory pattern recognition. We did this by having people rate how patterned various abstract art pieces were (think Jackson Pollack's work). Next, we had people report their belief in hell, the devil, and other negative beliefs, like demons and generational curses. After this, we asked people to indicate their willingness to engage in religiously taboo behaviors, like the Bloody Mary dare, using a Ouija board, visiting a psychic, reading the Satanic Bible, or participating in a séance. Finally, because research has found that religious people are also more superstitious, we had participants indicate their superstitious beliefs, such as knocking on wood for good luck or avoiding the number 13. We then compared religious dones with currently and never-religious individuals.

The results confirmed Sara's clinical observations: Religious dones were more likely than those who were never religious to hold negative religious beliefs, such as belief in hell, the devil, demons, supernatural forces, and generational curses. That is, we found evidence for religious residue for the darker side of religious belief. What's more, is that to the degree that religious dones held these negative beliefs, they were more likely to perceive illusory patterns, reported greater superstitious beliefs, and surprisingly reported greater willingness to engage in religious taboo behavior. Whereas the first two additional findings make sense, the third requires a bit more explanation: Why would religious dones be more likely to engage in forbidden behavior to the degree that they hold these negative beliefs? Shouldn't they be more anxious about them, as Sara and I are?

Although more research is certainly needed, perhaps a willingness to engage in previously off-limits behavior is a way of addressing those persistent fears head-on; what better way to convince yourself that you have nothing to fear than by doing the very things your religion promised would lead to peril and surviving unscathed. Or perhaps it's a kind of psychological reactance in the religious realm: Because you were raised being told you couldn't do these things, you now have permission to participate because you aren't inhibited by a religion you no longer follow. You may have witnessed people begin swearing more— a lot more—when they leave religion. The freedom of doing something that was forbidden can be enticing. Or maybe this pattern of endorsing religious taboo behavior reveals a way of trying to find new avenues for spiritual connection outside of the confines of religion.

To counter the potential criticism that perhaps these religious dones aren't "really done," we compared just the atheists dones and nones. Going beyond self-reported religious identity, we looked at people who reported no belief in God. The majority of dones and never religious (nones) reported no belief in God (85% and 92%, respectively), and examining those subsamples alone, we still find evidence for religious residue on negative religious beliefs. Disbelievers who were formerly religious reported greater belief in negative religious teachings, such as in the existence of Satan and hell, compared with those who were never religious. Indeed, people sooner give up their belief in God than their belief in hell or the devil.

Why might we see these persistent effects? A long-standing psychological truism is that bad is stronger than good. This means that there is an asymmetry in how we process negative information (Baumeister et al., 2001). We prioritize negative information; it carries more weight. This means it's more likely to get our attention, remain in our memories, affect our emotions, and alter our decisions. We remember the one negative thing our partner said far more and much longer than the several positive things they said. This cognitive prioritization of negative information makes sense from an evolutionary perspective. If we miss something positive in our environment, the consequences are relatively minor; we simply don't get the benefit of something good, but it's not catastrophic. On the other hand, if we miss something negative in our environment, such as a predator or angry member of another tribe, the consequences could be disastrous—or deadly. So, over time, the people who gave cognitive and attentional priority to positive events didn't survive as long as those who favored negative information. So, the negative process style was more adaptive and won out, and we're the descendants of those who cognitively prioritized negative information. And we, too, give more weight to the bad than the good.

Similarly, we might remember the negative features of our religious teachings and beliefs much longer than the positive ones because they are so potentially threatening. If you forget something about a blessing or some feature of the good life, it's not as detrimental as missing something about eternal conscious torment. You don't forget hell or the devil because the stakes are so high. Although more studies are needed, we might imagine that the negative parts of religion are stickier and more residual than the positive parts. It might be as hard as hell to shake one's belief in the devil.

WHY RELIGIOUS RESIDUE PERSISTS

We've seen the various ways in which former religious identification may continue to exert an effect after people walk away. But what are the mechanisms responsible for religious residue? There are three main pathways: the way you think, the habits you've formed, and the people you spend time with. Let's look at each of these.

First, religious residue persists because of cognitive factors—the way you've learned to think. Each of us processes information about our world using something researchers call *schemas*, which are mental frameworks. We develop schemas for many things in life, such as people we meet or situations we regularly encounter.

> *Schemas: Mental frameworks that help us make sense of the world.*

Schemas are really helpful for organizing information, directing our attention to what really matters in any given context, and shaping what we remember. Religion operates as a schema (McIntosh, 1995).

Why Does Religious Residue Exist?

- Because you have learned to process information from a religious framework.
- Because you have developed religion-based habits.
- Because your social world is largely religious.

It helps people interpret events in consistent ways and guides them to pay more attention to certain things and less attention to more peripheral information. For example, a religious schema might guide someone to perceive adversity as a "test from God" or suffering as "an opportunity for growth." The thorny thing about schemas is that they are notoriously resistant to change. Even when presented with counterattitudinal or schema-inconsistent evidence, such beliefs are enduring and persevere. We disregard information that doesn't fit within our schemas or make excuses for it; rather than change our schema, we ignore information that doesn't confirm our preexisting beliefs. The result is that we get rather entrenched in our schemas. And this process is especially potent for complex or elaborate schemas, where the beliefs are central to someone's identity—like religion.

The end result for religious residue is that if people were raised with a strong, central schema for religion, they are going to continue to interpret information in a schema-consistent manner, even if other aspects of their situation have changed. Deciding you no longer want to identify as religious doesn't suddenly make it easier to see the world through a new lens. Instead, what most people find is that their internal cognitive processing doesn't match their external identity, which can lead to considerable cognitive dissonance, anxiety, guilt, anger, or frustration. Externally, you may want to walk completely away from religion, but your cognitive machinery is still operating the way it has in the past: as a religious follower. And despite your best efforts to immerse yourself in experiences that run counter to your religious schema, these stubborn ways of seeing the world are difficult to change. Thus, you may continue to view and explain the world in religious terms, which can feel inconsistent and inauthentic.

A second reason religious residue persists is because many religious rituals and behaviors become habits. *Habits* are internalized knowledge structures in which people rely on ritualistic behavioral patterns in particular settings (Aarts & Dijksterhuis, 2000). Put more simply, habits become automatic responses in conditioned contexts. If you always prayed before enjoying your meal, you might find yourself bowing your head and closing your eyes before taking your first bite of food despite no longer being religious. Or if attending a religious service was a central rhythm in your weekend schedule, you might feel compelled to wake up and go to church on Sunday morning despite having left the faith. These behavioral patterns leave deep grooves that are hard to escape. Sometimes, our body even responds to situational cues before we're consciously aware that we're acting. As we make associations (e.g., prayer with meals, religious gatherings on specific days, religious rituals at certain times of day), we implicitly anticipate these regular associations and begin to move subconsciously toward these ingrained behaviors. And just as habits take a considerable amount of time to form, they take quite a bit of time and effort to change. Indeed, the development of religious habits may persist even once one's outward identity has changed.

Religion is rich with rituals. These regular ritualized behaviors mean that religion etches strong patterns in our functioning, making it hard to break free from these repetitive responses. Many times, these habitualized reactions occur so quickly, and automatically, that our conscious mind is trying to catch up to our initial response. And for those who have left religion, they might find that their first instinct (a religious habit) no longer matches their external religious identity or desired behavior. For me, I instinctually prayed immediately every time I flew on a plane, before my flight took off. It became a superstition, where I felt that if I didn't do it, something terrible would happen. It was a ritual that rang hollow, devoid of any real meaning other than a psychological safety blanket, but even as my own beliefs changed, it was hard to get rid of this behavior. Eventually, I took a gamble and didn't compulsively rattle off my superstitious prayer before takeoff. When we landed safely, I exhaled a sigh of relief. And over time, this superstitious habit waned, but it was a hard pattern to break.

A third reason why religious residue may linger is because of our communities—who we spend time with. Social factors play a large role in maintaining religious belief and behavior, so *religious communities* may contribute to residue effects of religion. When people are embedded in religious communities, they think, feel, and act like religious people. My own research on both morality and consumer behavior found that the more frequently religious dones interacted with religious individuals, the greater the religious residue effect (DeWall & Van Tongeren, 2022; Van Tongeren, DeWall, Hardy, et al., 2021). Continuing to engage with religious communities may translate to a strong effect of one's religious past. After all, it's hard to form a new identity, and live out that identity authentically and fully, if you still feel the pull of a previous identity and the expectations of a prior community. To the degree that your social world is still largely religious, and full of religious individuals, you may find that your previous religious identity continues to loom large.

Practically, many people who leave religion still have rather strong religious social ties and communities. Many religious dones have family members who are strongly religious, especially if they grew up in a home where religion was centrally important. Similarly, religious communities are often a source of friendships and other social connections, which means that religious dones may also have plenty of friends and acquaintances who are religious. This network of religious people amplifies the religious residue of the power of one's previous religious identity. Because of this, religious dones often feel caught between two worlds: the previous religious world from which they came but with whom they no longer identify and a new, but perhaps lonelier and more isolated, nonreligious world where they must forge new friendships and social connections. And for many good reasons, plenty of religious dones continue to maintain their religious communities and stay in connection with plenty of religious people (after all, currently many people in the United States are religious), which can extend the effects of religious residue. Other times, religious dones seek community with other dones, which can be reassuring; it can be helpful to find support among other people who have walked away from faith. However, if the main (or only) thing you talk about when you get together is religion, it may ironically continue to keep you embedded in those religious tendencies you're working hard to alter. Even if your social interactions focus more on religion's ills than benefits, it's still centering your time and attention on religion, which may keep religion (and its residue) top of mind.

LIVING WITH THE RESIDUE

Religious residue is a widespread phenomenon. Of note, these studies don't suggest that this residue is good or bad, nor do they suggest that it's maladaptive if you experience religious residue. Rather, this research reveals that across cultures, religion persists after walking away. It affects people of different ages, from different cultures, and of different genders. Certainly, other factors will contribute to the degree to which religion persists, including the nature and content of one's religious upbringing. For example, if you were raised a very strict, conservative (perhaps fundamentalist) home where religion was the central and defining feature of your identity, you're likely going to experience a much stronger degree of religious residue than those for whom their religious identity was merely nominal or those raised in home where religion was more peripheral. One of my friends who was nominally religious was only minimally affected after leaving religion; in fact, he appreciated the extra time to play golf each Sunday morning. But his wife, who grew up extremely religious, was more strongly affected. She had a harder time letting go of her religious upbringing and felt the persistent residue more acutely. Similarly, if your view of religion consisted of strongly negative features, such as a menacing devil who sought to tempt you into decisions that would lead to your eventual eternal and irrevocable damnation, it might be rather hard to shake such threatening beliefs. So, although religious residue is pervasive and cross-cultural, it is also contextually dependent, and some of you might experience it to a greater degree than others.

How do you live with this persistent residue, especially if your goal is to develop a life of meaning and flourishing apart from religion? Research offers some helpful insights. First, understanding that religious residue is common and widespread can help normalize the process of feeling the continued effects of religion after leaving the faith (Van Tongeren, DeWall, Chen, et al., 2021). If you feel like you can't shake religion, you're not alone. Many (if not most) people feel this way. There is nothing wrong with you; you're trying to make a significant change in your life by altering a powerful schema, paired with deeply etched habits while being embedded in a social community that promotes your previous religious way of thinking and acting. That's quite a tall order. A change process this monumental will take time. To borrow some religious language, don't be afraid to give yourself some grace. Patience is your friend in this journey.

But remember that research also provides some context and limitations for this effect: Religious residue does decay (Van Tongeren, DeWall, Hardy, et al., 2021). The effects of religion wane over time. It is unlikely that religious residue persists as strongly 10 years after deidentification as it did a few months after walking away from religion.

How to Live With Religious Residue

- Be patient with yourself. Religious residue is common and widespread, and the effects will eventually mostly subside.
- Identify the places where religious residue shows up in your life (thoughts, feelings, and behaviors).
- Make conscious behavioral changes. The more you make them, the less religious residue will "stick."

However, some residue will linger. Knowing that the effects of religion will subside can help you endure what might feel like an anxiety-provoking and frustrating time of cognitive dissonance, as will accepting the reality that even once you feel as though you have fully left religion, your religious past may continue to surface in unexpected ways. This is a normal psychological process.

Second, as you become more aware of the process of religious residue, you can start identifying the places it continues to show up in your life. On the one hand, this may look like persistent feelings of guilt and shame associated with religion. When hearing about my research on people leaving religion, a colleague of mine retorted, "As my mom always said, 'once a Catholic, always a Catholic.'" When I pried a bit more for some context, he revealed that even though he had left his faith long ago, there were some parts of his religious upbringing—largely around shame and guilt—that he couldn't shake. He still felt as though religion's shadow loomed large around moral decisions and how to best live his life. Even as an ardent disbeliever, he felt like the stronghold religion maintained in his ethical and moral center couldn't be fully shaken. It still guided his actions. He argued that "Catholic guilt" was real and lasting. You, too, might continue to feel these lingering negative emotions.

On the other hand, religious residue may express itself in your new ways of thinking and behaving. Religious residue can be sneaky and may masquerade as change. Even if you've left your conservative fundamental values behind, you may be drawn to strong, severe belief systems with different content (something we'll talk about more later in the book). Similarly, you may seek religious teachers or spiritual gurus to tell you what to believe and how to live, outsourcing these responsibilities as you may have been accustomed to. Or you may continue to wait for a "savior" to change your life circumstances or save you from misery, when actionable change is available to you if you take ownership and make different decisions. But these may really be expressions of religious residue taking shape in your new life: replacing a pastor figure with a spiritual life coach or shunning all-or-nothing beliefs only to throw yourself headlong into a new belief system (perhaps even diametrically opposed to religion) that leaves little room to doubt, question, or entertain alternative perspectives. Realizing that these patterns run deep can help people begin to choose lives based on autonomy, authenticity, and their values, rather than being overwhelmed by, or reacting against, their religious history.

Finally, consciously making behavioral changes will cause some of this residue to subside. Begin by asking yourself, "Am I doing this because it's a value of mine, or because it's a habit that feels comfortable?" Making changes is anxiety-provoking (like ceasing a superstitious plane protection prayer), but creating new habits requires shifting from a familiar religious groove to one more aligned with your values. Over time, with continued practice, you may eventually find yourself less reactive to these lingering vestiges of your previous religious faith. Depending on your reason for leaving religion and your current attitude toward religious people and religion in general, small reminders or subtle nudges that betray your former religious identity may simply be milestones of your identity development. You might notice how an ingrained response no longer fits and now feels rather foreign, which can serve as an indicator of how different your new identity is. In fact, you may come to find rare occurrences of religious residue as a marker of the growth you've experienced and how far away your religious identity now feels.

Religious residue isn't something to be embarrassed about nor is it an indicator that you're never going to be able to craft a new, meaningful identity apart from religion. Rather, it's a normal part of making a significant identity change apart from religion and endeavoring to develop a new set of beliefs and behaviors in a new social community. The lingering effects represent the growing pains of an authentic existential journey.

CHAPTER 5

SEARCHING FOR MEANING IN THE EXISTENTIAL CHASM

In the weeks that followed September 11, 2001, many Americans sought to make sense of an unspeakable tragedy. Thousands of Americans had been killed, and the rest of the country (and many around the world) grappled with understanding what happened and why. Political commentators turned toward explanations that affirmed their political leanings. Religious leaders similarly followed their theological inclinations, invoking God's will or wrath as playing a role in the horrific events. One of the most notable public reactions was made by Jerry Falwell, who was speaking with Pat Robertson on his show, *The 700 Club*. Falwell asserted that the godlessness of America—most conspicuously expressed by the existence of pro-choice individuals, feminists, and members of the LGBTQ+ community—caused this to happen. Robertson agreed. Other Christian evangelical leaders interpreted the events similarly, blaming a departure from God for the horrors of the terrorist attack. To be sure, their claims did not necessarily capture widespread religious sentiment, but it did illustrate how people turn toward religious teachings to try to interpret and explain seemingly chaotic or difficult life events. And while it bolstered some people's religious commitments and strengthened their faith, it drove others away from religion, as they sought to distance themselves from any intimation that they, too, would share these beliefs or be associated with that dogma.

Certainly, this was not the first instance of people relying on their religious worldview to make sense of tragedy nor was it the last. Hurricanes, earthquakes, pandemics (including the 2020 coronavirus outbreak), and other mass suffering have been viewed as divine retribution or interpreted in ways that bolster people's religious teachings. Often, minoritized groups are the focus of these scapegoating theories, which perpetuates prejudice and does little to sway public opinion in favor of religion.

The human desire to make sense of adversity and suffering is not confined solely to religion. Falwell and Robertson were not unique in their desire to apply an explanatory framework to a disconcerting and threatening event in hopes of making sense of tragedy. Rather, the motivation to perceive life in meaningful ways, and indeed our life as inherently meaningful, is a natural part of being human. Each of us does this naturally and automatically every day in ways large and small. Usually, we take for granted these mental scripts we rely on to make sense of the world around us, and it's not until something larger, more unsettling, chaotic, or threatening emerges that we can more clearly see how we rely on a constellation of beliefs to effectively process the world around us. This is because we humans are meaning-making animals: Our brains are hardwired for making meaning.

THE HUMAN NEED FOR MEANING

We humans have a fundamental need for meaning. This desire shows up in how we think and process information, the views we hold about ourselves and other people, and the behaviors we enact throughout our day (Park, 2010). In fact, some have even argued this drive for meaning is the central, unifying motivation that explains most of why humans do what they do (Heine et al., 2006). I think that our desire for meaning helps explain why people are religious and can offer important insights into navigating the process of religious change.

Evidence for the need for meaning comes from various lines of research. One of the clearest arguments for our desire to perceive ourselves and our lives as meaningful is garnered from a wide literature demonstrating that we naturally defend meaning. Because we are so strongly motivated to seek meaning in our lives, we have assembled a quite sophisticated set of strategies to maintain that meaning when it is under threat. Researchers have called this many things—such as compensation, self-protection, or affirmation—but they all converge on the same idea of strategic defensiveness (Heine et al., 2006). We protect meaning at all costs.

The basic idea is something like this: Meaning is an important part of human life. When one area of our life experiences a loss of meaning—such as a blow to our self-esteem, a lack of certainty around a decision, a rupture in a relationship, or reminders of our finitude—we begin to affirm other areas of meaning as a compensatory response to this threat. We do this strategically. Because these different domains all contribute to our perceived sense of meaning, being unable to find meaning in one area often results in us shifting to find meaning in other areas. For example, when people are stressed about things they cannot control (e.g., an uncertain decision at work, waiting to hear back after a medical test), they often either focus on those things that they can control (e.g., cleaning their house, attempting to control other people's behaviors) or double down on other sources of meaning (e.g., investing more in their relationships, seeking approval and self-esteem). This process maintains our vitally important sense of meaning in life.

This process often happens automatically and unconsciously. One of my first studies in graduate school revealed that when people's meaning in life is threatened subconsciously (e.g., flashing words too quickly to be consciously recognized on a computer screen), they reported more meaning in life than those who weren't threatened (Van Tongeren & Green, 2010). And when we interviewed participants after the study, virtually no one was aware that their meaning was being undermined. This process happened outside of conscious awareness. Defensiveness is our default.

We also remake meaning after adversity and loss. For example, whenever we have trouble making sense of the world around us, or there is a mismatch between our belief about the way the world should work and the ways things actually happened, we experience distress proportionate to that discrepancy (Park, 2010). The bigger the discrepancy, the worse we feel—and the more meaning-making efforts we have to pursue to restore our sense of meaning. We usually do this in two ways. Namely, we either adjust our beliefs to fit reality or change our interpretation of reality to fit into our beliefs. The former takes a lot of work and is cognitively challenging, so many times, the easier (and more common) response is to change how we make sense of events to fit into our preexisting cognitive frameworks. Leaving religion is often different. Many times, we simply can't reinterpret events in ways that are consistent with our (religious) beliefs, so we end up changing them altogether. This means shattered assumptions and may contribute to a significant source of stress. And it leaves us searching for a new way to explain the world.

WHAT IS MEANING?

It's important to understand what meaning is. Although it can feel tricky to define something as broad as meaning in life, researchers have converged on a definition that includes three parts: coherence, significance, and purpose (George & Park, 2016; Martela & Steger, 2016). Put differently, we perceive that life has meaning when it

Searching for Meaning in Adversity and Loss

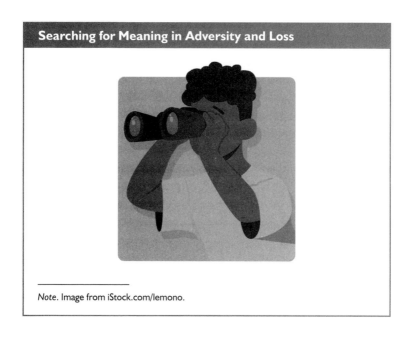

Note. Image from iStock.com/lemono.

makes sense, we matter, and we can connect with something bigger than ourselves.

Coherence is the cognitive part of meaning in life, and it describes the feeling when things make sense. When we explain why something happens by fitting it into our preconceived ideas of how the world should work, life feels pretty meaningful. Senseless suffering, adversity, or unexplained events often threaten our coherence and ability to meaningfully explain why something happened. Religion is often a powerful source of coherence because it offers rich and comprehensive explanations of the world around us, demarcating good and evil, and offering clear guidelines for how to live a moral life. It provides a lens through which people can interpret events as part of a larger cosmic narrative or story.

Significance is the social part of meaning in life, and it describes the feeling of mattering. When we feel that we are people of worth

---

Sources of Meaning

- Help us make sense of life.
- Make us feel like we matter.
- Provide a purpose.

---

and value and that other people care deeply about us, life is brimming with meaning. Significance can also arise when we feel as though we are making a difference—contributing to the world in a powerful way. Someone or something loves us, and perhaps needs us, and we matter to them. Religion can be a strong source of significance. Religious people often feel as though they matter greatly, given that many believe God created them, communicates with them, lives inside them, has imbued them with a divine spirit or spark, or may have even died for them. How much more could one matter than by having a loving relationship with the most powerful entity in all of existence?

Purpose is the motivational part of meaning in life, and it describes the feeling of having a goal or connection with something larger than ourselves. It's the sense that we know what we are doing with our lives and our energy is directed toward something outside ourselves: a cause, a calling, or a creative expression. It's a feeling of transcending the ordinary mundanity of daily life and escaping the confines of the self. It fills us with passion and energy and makes it possible for us to reach our human potential. Many religious people seek desperately for God's plan or calling on their lives or may orient their lives around a set of religious teachings. Others dedicate themselves to spreading their religious teachings to others and trying to persuade or convert others to join their religious group. Still others find purpose by upholding the moral mandates of their religion as part of a quest for a good life now, and a better life after death.

WHERE DOES MEANING COME FROM?

A few different social psychological theories highlight the human drive for meaning and have suggested different sources of meaning. One theory is the meaning maintenance model, which suggests that various social motivations all serve the same superordinate goal of making life meaningful (Heine et al., 2006). For example, they reason that our desire for self-esteem, our craving for certainty, our need to belong, and our quest for symbolic immortality are all in service of a broader ambition to imbue this life with meaning. In addition, proponents of this theory argue our desire for meaning is so pervasive, and humans so naturally meaning-makers, that when we experience a loss of meaning in one area, we're quick to compensate for that meaning in another area. So when our self-esteem takes a knock after our work presentation is poorly received, we're more likely to seek meaning in our relationship with our partner as a way to regain equilibrium (and more sensitive to potential rejection as another loss). Or when we're uncertain about the future while waiting to hear if we got a new job, we're more likely to protect our ego and seek affirmation to enhance our self-esteem. Let's unpack each of these domains of meaning and see how they relate to the process of religious change.

First, a primary source of meaning is self-esteem. We can think of self-esteem as our global evaluation of ourselves. Simply, it's the attitude we hold toward ourselves. If we view ourselves as having worth and value, we likely have higher self-esteem. Our self-esteem can come from external sources, such as the positive feelings we get when we garner the approval or affirmation of others, accomplish something notable, or outperform other people, or it can arise from internal sources, such as believing that we have inherent value without any regard to our achievements or the validation of other people. Regardless of where we find our self-esteem, research has suggested that feelings of self-esteem are related to perceiving life as meaningful. In fact, healthy and adaptive coping following trauma or suffering is often marked by a self-esteem and feelings of positive self-worth (Taylor, 1983). So according to the meaning maintenance model, our drive for self-esteem is motivated largely by our need for meaning in life.

Religion offers its devotees a strong sense of self-esteem. Although for many, they view this esteem as contingent on external standards (e.g., living up to the morals and teachings of one's religion), it can be rather powerful to believe that we ourselves are imbued with a divine spirit, have a connection with a powerful deity or God, or are the reason why God interacts with humanity. After all, the belief that the creator of the universe loves you so deeply is likely to translate to a healthy dose of self-esteem. As the teaching goes, if God is for me, who can be against me? Of course, as I noted, for many, this self-esteem is tenuous. It depends on (unflinchingly high) standards of religion, and many feel ill-equipped to live up to the moral perfection required in many religions. This can lead to feelings of shame and guilt when people are unable to attain that degree of moral behavior.

It is also important to consider that lack of religion can undermine self-esteem as well. To the degree that people feel special and loved by believing in an interactive, benevolent supernatural deity who relates with them and cares deeply about their daily life,

---

How Religion Gives Us Meaning

- It offers a sense of self-esteem.
- It appeals to our desire for certainty and closure.
- It offers opportunities for relationships and belonging.
- It promises immortality.

the absence of that belief may erode self-esteem. People may feel as though they don't matter and as if their life is less meaningful (or perhaps even meaningless) as they transition away from religion. Abandoning the belief that you are part of God's special plan can leave people feeling empty and alone. After all, if you believed, like the Blues Brothers, that you're "on a mission from God," letting go of a special purpose for your life can feel deflating, disheartening, or downright depressing. It's a steep drop of meaning.

A second resource for meaning is our desire for certainty and closure. Life is easier—and feels more meaningful—when we're able to predict the world around us (Heintzelman & King, 2014). We have a strong propensity to believe that we are right, and we feel more comfortable when we can explain the world around us. This is why we seek out familiar structure and cognitive closure, rather than leaving things unknown or uncertain. Although each of us differ in how this looks personally, most of us desire to make sense of the world in ways that are consistent with our beliefs. And when we can do that, life feels pretty meaningful. This means our desire for predictability, the reason why we crave certainty and closure, is because it provides us with a sense of meaning. This is a primary reason why the global health pandemic of 2020 was so upsetting. Not only did it pose a mortal threat to many in the early stages before vaccines or treatments were developed, it also revealed to all of us that life is wildly unpredictable and could change rapidly. It shattered our illusions of control.

Religions tend to offer a strong degree of certainty and closure. Many of them proffer an absolute account for the nature of humanity, the world around us, and the pathway toward living a good life (and perhaps vanquishing suffering and death). In fact, many religions claim to offer the "truth" among a vast array of competing lesser nontruths or falsehoods. Although many religions are indeed based on the premise of faith, or placing one's trust in a deity (or, in more recent history, a set of religious teachings or doctrinal claims about that deity), they promise a degree of certainty that one is indeed correct by holding those faithful beliefs. This certainty is proposed to provide a better version of this life and, for some, life everlasting after death. This is particularly true of certain instantiations of religion, such as Christian fundamentalism, which vault absolute and unwavering confidence in one's beliefs as the chief virtue (and signal) of faithful followership. In such cases, doubt is not only discouraged but often seen as an indicator of sin or spiritual weakness that must be eradicated.

For many people, the process of leaving religion begins with seeing cracks in the certainty with which people hold their beliefs. Some people come to understand that they cannot be absolutely certain about their claims about this life and the next, and even the most compelling evidence for one's beliefs always involves some degree of trust or faith, whether such beliefs are religious or not. For example, even the simple act of sitting in chair to read a book requires doing quick mental calculus that you believe that chair is sufficiently constructed to hold your weight and support you as you enjoy some leisure reading. You trust or have faith it will hold you. Similarly, we trust or have faith that our spouses are faithful and loving, our doctors are competent, and our children are telling us the truth. We can never know for sure, so we trust, based on sufficiently strong evidence. Some people realize they can never really know for sure if their religion is true, and the mere claim that one's religion is unassailably true and beyond question feels disruptive and dishonest. And when they begin to have doubts, whether those are generated because of personal experience or intellectual questioning, it ironically becomes unacceptable in some religious spaces, which creates distance between themselves and their religious identity. The more they question, the less they feel their religious structures can bear the weight of such questions, and they break—leaving the person uncertain, without closure, and swimming in a sea of groundlessness. The faith they put in their previous beliefs has come up wanting, and they begin to look for new sources of certainty or closure. A third wellspring of meaning, and one that may be the most obvious, is our desire for relationships and belonging. Of course, from an evolutionary perspective, belonging is advantageous for survival and necessary for reproduction, but this strong motivation also serves more transcendent goals. Most people agree that the most meaningful aspect of their lives is their relationships. Our need to belong, fit in, be liked and accepted, and have other people include us likely serves the broader drive for meaning. This need to belong often means that rejection and ostracism feel terrible, undermine our well-being, and may lead to aggression. Accordingly, we seek the validation and support of others, and we may even maintain relationships with people who may not be healthy or kind because we fear abandonment and isolation, arguing that a mediocre (or poor) relationship may be better than no relationship at all. This is also one of the reasons why ruptures in relationships or familial strain can feel so stressful and why efforts to repair relationships, such as forgiveness, can help restore meaning (Van Tongeren et al., 2015). Our need for belonging and meaning go hand-in-hand.

Religion is a highly social enterprise. The root word of religion is *religio*, which means "to-bind," suggesting that religion helps bind us to other people (and to God). Religious communities are often the features of the faith that people love the most while they are religious and miss the most when they are gone. Being surrounded by a caring group of like-minded people who will bake you a casserole when your aunt passes away is powerfully supportive, just as being ostracized or rejected by the same group because of your beliefs, actions, or identity can feel deeply painful and isolating. Being part of a religious community can make life feel incredibly meaningful and leaving that community can undermine our sense of meaning in profound ways. It is easy to underestimate the psychological benefits of being able to join a community where you assume many people think or believe in ways similar to you, are likely to treat you (mostly) kindly because of a shared set of values, and are motivated to maintain harmonious group relationships. For example, joining a church or temple or mosque when moving to a new city is a form of fast-tracking community building and relational development. This kind of social support is one of the strongest appeals of religion.

Church support can vary. When my brother passed away, we weren't actively part of a church, but we had a strong religious community. We used to get together each week, share a meal, and pray for each other. When I lost my brother, this group came together for us in ways I'm still grateful for. They delivered meals, spent time with us, took us out for a beer, cried with us, and one time even cleaned our house. It was so powerful that we started attending the local church where many of them went. On the other hand, my wife and I were deeply invested in a different church for many years when my dad became ill. He slowly worsened over a period of 6 months, which was a considerable source of sorrow and stress for us both. We had hoped that our religious community would offer support; after all, we saw how they celebrated births and rallied around others who were in need. We participated in numerous meal shares, cooking up countless lasagnas and delivering them to fellow congregants. But when my dad was in his final weeks, our church community was painfully absent. One of the best parts of religion suddenly went missing, and it felt like the floor fell out from beneath us.

In a similar fashion, this means leaving religion often involves a significant loss to one's felt sense of community. Many people who walk away from faith often feel isolated and alone. In fact, recent research suggests that religious dones often conceal their nonreligious identity in highly religious cultures (Mackey et al., 2023).

Of course, for many, their felt sense of community and acceptance from their religious community was indeed conditional, based on what they believed, how they acted, or their particular identity, and many are experiencing real rejection and judgment. For others, the felt absence of a religious community is painful, even if that community no longer represents the kind of people with whom we'd like to commune. For example, although many religious fundamentalist groups are harsh, judgmental, and severe, they also have a fierce sense of community and loyalty, and those who were once part of these communities grieve the lost camaraderie of sharing life with a set of other people who were deeply invested and involved in each other's lives.

The last source of meaning identified is what researchers call symbolic immortality, which is our belief that we will be remembered, or live on in the memory of others, after we die (Pyszczynski et al., 2015). People seek this memorialization in many ways: through their careers or work, by artistic or creative contributions, via philanthropic donations to causes or buildings or organizations that bear their name, or in having children who will carry on one's name and legacy. When we appreciate the work done by others, listen to music composed by a talented artist, walk through the hospital wing bearing the name of a generous donor, or think of the memory that children carry of their parents (or grandparents), a little bit of that person continues to live on, carried in our hearts and minds. It's as if a part of them is still here, continuing on, alive as they once were. Symbolic immortality helps sidestep the looming problem of death. After all, it allows us to believe we're making a significant and lasting difference in the world and that we, too, shall be remembered. It's the salve to the frightening realization that we're a momentary blip in the universe. And when we feel like we will be remembered and our work or legacy or investment in others or making the world a better place will carry on, we feel as though our life is meaningful.

Religion not only wonderfully offers symbolic immortality, it offers an upgrade: literal immortality. What better way to vanquish a fear of death than to overcome death altogether? You cannot be forgotten if you never die, are reincarnated or born again, or are able to achieve eternal life. By transforming the finality of death into a pause—between this life and the next—religion offers a sense of immortality that no other worldview can: permanence. According to some religions, we will never be extinguished. Now, other religions, such as Buddhism, contend that once we reach nirvana, we will indeed be extinguished and our cycle of suffering will end, but even in doing so, such beliefs eradicate the fear of death and imbue this life with meaning: The goal is to improve in the next life to reach a desired end-state. We have a purpose. Our lives have meaning and value. We know how we should be spending our time in this life, and if we do it right, people will remember us.

Walking away from religion can mean leaving behind these promises of immortality. Although there are still other ways of seeking symbolic immortality, such efforts may feel like cheap substitutes after once believing that you can achieve the "real thing." Sure, it may be nice to live on in the minds and hearts of others because of how you lived your life, but wouldn't it be better to actually live on by achieving eternal life? Religion has cornered the market on literal immortality, so leaving that behind can undermine meaning in profound ways. Death becomes a fresh fear and new reality. After deidentification, you might feel a combination of regret for having spent a portion of your life—your only life—following a religion you no longer believe, mixed with the anxiety that accompanies a heightened awareness that life is short and will end with all finality when you die, which could be at any moment. The "salvation safety net" is gone, and you have to face the reality that everything could be over for good without warning. It can be a downright terrifying experience to endure. And it's more common than you might think.

DEVELOPING MEANING: CULTURAL WORLDVIEWS

One of the primary ways that we form meaning is through the development and maintenance of cultural worldviews. *Cultural worldviews* are mental frameworks for making sense of the world around us (i.e., offering coherence), demarcating the value of human life (i.e., granting significance), and orienting us toward something larger than ourselves (i.e., providing purpose). They are a constellation of beliefs that offer clear explanations for the nature of humanity, how people should live and relate to each other, and, in many cases, what happens to us after we die. They include beliefs about morality, customs, norms, and how to behave. They are the lenses through which we make sense of and explain the world around us. For example, people of two different political persuasions will interpret the same event differently, such as both perceiving that their respective candidate performed better in a political debate. These frameworks are culturally dependent and socially validated, meaning we're often rewarded by others for upholding the standards of our cultural worldview and may be punished when we don't act in accord with their values. This approval usually results in feelings of self-esteem and inclusion, both of which are psychologically rewarding.

Cultural worldviews take a number of forms, such as politics, nationalism, or—perhaps chief among all—religion. Each of these do provide a sense of coherence, significance, and purpose, but I think religions stand apart from other cultural worldviews in their meaning-providing efficacy. More specifically, I think religions are particularly effective as cultural worldviews because of their certainty, content, and comprehensiveness. Let's examine each of these briefly.

First, relative to other cultural worldviews, religions offer a particular degree of certainty. Many religions make exclusive epistemic claims and warn followers that alternative perspectives are misinformed at best and deceitful at worst. Because they assert absolute truth, religious followers can know "for certain" that their beliefs are correct. This degree of certainty is a powerful remedy to anxiety and helps individuals cope with stress and adversity. Moreover, it operates like a built-in safety device from pundits or critics: Those who impugn religious worldviews are woefully deceived and should be ignored. This creates a self-affirming cycle of disregarding information that challenges one's religious worldview and instead focusing only on other certainty-enhancing evidence. After all, you're psychologically rewarded for holding some beliefs, like the afterlife, with plenty of certainty to manage the doubt that arises from a lack of sure evidence. And this certainty leaves little room for disbelief both inside and outside of the ranks; even believers can experience shame and guilt for questioning.

A second feature that makes religion unique is the content of the beliefs. Many of the features of religious belief evoke transcendent connection with a supernatural agent or agents, which can provide people with a deep sense of significance and purpose. Whereas political or nationalistic worldviews describe what happens in this life, religious worldviews extend to the next life as well. When people feel as though they are part of a greater cosmic plan, they feel more important and meaningful. In fact, some have argued that religious meaning is perceived to be more meaningful than other sources of meaning (Newton & McIntosh, 2013). After all, one's calling from God must be more important than one's career or relationships, right? And if one's actions are divinely inspired, they likely are also sanctioned as morally correct. Religious worldviews have a different flavor because their content is unique.

Finally, religious worldviews are comprehensive. They cover the totality of human life, from the origins of the universe to what happens after we die. They explain a range of the human condition that no other worldview can, including creation myths, moral codes, and the afterlife. To be sure, religion may posit to explain nearly everything we experience as humans. That's a bold claim, and one not offered by many other explanatory frameworks (perhaps with the exception of science for some, although I think science and religion ask very different questions). And it's this comprehensiveness that can make religion so appealing and so difficult to shake—as well as nearly impossible to replace.

So each of has a cultural worldview that provides us with a meaningful way of engaging with and understanding the world around us. These worldviews provide us with maps of making sense of events, achieving significance, and finding our purpose. Religion is one of the most potent cultural worldviews at providing people with a sense of meaning, making it particularly challenging to replace after people walk away from religion. In fact, one of the reasons why people may struggle leaving religion is because it is a powerful source of meaning in life and the coherence it provides.

Let's pause and take stock. In this chapter, we've discussed that (a) we humans have a fairly strong drive for meaning, (b) which comes in the form of coherence, significance, and purpose (c) that likely supersedes or subsumes some other social motivations, including our strivings for self-esteem, the desire for certainty and closure, our need to belong, and our quest for symbolic immortality, and (d) religious worldviews do an excellent job of providing meaning across those domains. It also suggests that when we leave religion, we might struggle to find meaning in the same way religion offered it to us. But does leaving religion really mean life feels less meaningful?

PAYING THE MEANING PENALTY

Last chapter, we discussed religious residue, or the tendency for the cognitive, emotional, and behavioral effects of religion to linger long after people deidentify. We see this in research where religious dones look more like currently religious individuals on a host of outcome variables than do those who were never religious. Given consistent evidence for this phenomenon, I was curious whether it extended to meaning in life. After all, if religion provides people with a sense of meaning, would those who left religion still benefit from the residue effects of their previous identity? Might religious dones report higher meaning than those who were never religious?

I had included a widely used measure of meaning in life in several studies I was running that included current, former, and never religious individuals (Van Tongeren et al., in press). The cross-cultural evidence was revealing. There is no evidence for religious residue on meaning in life. In fact, religious dones report significantly lower meaning in life compared to religious individuals—comparable to those who have never been religious. Although more research is needed to confirm this conclusion, it suggests that life loses meaning after leaving religion.

Of course, it could be that religious dones first felt a perceived loss of meaning in life and then decided to deidentify from religion, but that wouldn't quite explain why those who were never religious also have lower meaning in life. Rather, it seems more plausible (and likely) that religion is a strong source of meaning in life, and those who are not religious do not draw as deep of a sense of meaning. Put differently, after walking away from religion, religious dones pay a meaning penalty. Indeed, life feels less meaningful.

Religion is uniquely positioned to provide meaning across the various domains of self-esteem, certainty, belonging, and (symbolic) immortality. But more broadly, religion also provides higher order meaning. When we're investing in a belief system that purports that a loving supernatural agent or deity is overseeing, and perhaps directing, our daily affairs, life takes on supreme meaning. Not only do my mundane events become meaningful in the service of a larger goal, but I discern my life's calling and pursue it passionately. The heavens are ordered in a beautiful arrangement that conveys intention, care, and purpose. Even random events are merely viewed as such because of my limited understanding (remember how religious folks are more likely to see patterns, as we found in the study on hell?). Everything is held together by a bigger plan, a greater meaning— The Greater Meaning.

When this is stripped away, people are often left viewing the world as cold, indifferent, and uncaring. The universe is a set of random events that managed to co-occur to create life—not out of benevolence and intention, but accidentally—because any other way would not have yielded the conditions necessary for life. Some view existence not as a loving creation but a lucky accident, a by-product. The certainty and finality of death often render life an absurd joke, robbing any lasting or permanent meaning from human existence. Indeed, there is no bigger plan or greater meaning at all. In fact, the truth is that there is simply meaninglessness everywhere. The only part that some religions got right, some argue, is that "everything is meaningless."

What this means is that a lot of people fall into a nihilistic despair after leaving religion. Their structured way of seeing, and relating to the world, has been shattered, and they must find new ways to create meaning. They've experienced a drop in meaning. If there is no more absolute truth, no set of religiously inspired moral teachings worth following, or any loving supernatural agent that cares or interacts with me, what is the point of this life? If it all ends and I'm certainly going to be forgotten, how can I have any more meaning than an overripe avocado or a sack of marbles? If The Greater Meaning is indeed a myth, doesn't that suggest all meaning is a myth?

And although nihilism is a common response, it's not usually a sustainable response. That is, it's a way station, not the final destination. And there are three reasons. First, as we've discussed, people need meaning in their lives. Without it, we languish. Our mental health depends on crafting meaningful narratives of our lives and finding meaning in suffering (Van Tongeren & Showalter Van Tongeren,

123

2020). And while some get stuck in nihilistic rumination for years, nearly everyone will begin to find new pathways toward meaning. Second, nihilism itself can become someone's source of meaning. Ironically, believing that nothing has meaning is a way of making sense of the world, which provides people with some degree of certainty and closure—and, thus, meaning. When we expect the worst or see everything as random, and our beliefs are confirmed, life begins to feel a bit more predictable. So even our commitment to a meaningless nihilism provides us with a modicum of meaning. And finally, we usually jostle free from nihilism because we humans are relentless meaning-makers. When we feel threatened, our natural and automatic response is to restore meaning in other areas. Our default is to find new sources of meaning. It's hardwired into our cognitive architecture. So, over time, you will find a way out from the shadow of nihilism and the disbelief of meaning. More likely than not, however, how you find your meaning and make sense of the world will be quite different, and it might not lead to the same overall level of meaning as when you were religious. But most every religious done has to pay the meaning penalty first. It seems that Jean-Paul Sartre was correct when he asserted: "Life has no meaning the moment you lose the illusion of being eternal."

FINDING NEW MEANING

Leaving religion requires us to find new pathways toward meaning. No longer available are religion's ready answers for making sense of the world, achieving mattering or significance, or drawing on a grander cosmic plan or purpose. Of course, as you experience the loss of meaning associated with walking away from religion, you'll naturally start seeking out new sources of meaning. The drive for meaning will motivate you to craft new ways of explaining the world around you, of understanding your worth and value, and seeking to find a fulfilling and transcendent purpose. But just how does this process take place? And perhaps more importantly, why does this process often feel so difficult? To fully understand the challenges of finding new meaning requires that we take a closer look at some of the harsher realities of what it means to be human. We must confront the existential chasm.

THE EXISTENTIAL CHASM

After leaving religion, the hardest thing you might have to navigate as a religious done is something I call the *existential chasm*. It's the cognitive realization and psychological state that arise from forfeiting formerly satisfactory answers offered by religion for existential questions and facing afresh the pressing concerns of human existence. It's the intellectual acknowledgment and complex set of emotions that accompany giving up your religious answers to existential questions and perceiving a gap in the ability for your new meaning systems to address these concerns as fully as religion once did.

Each of us have to come to terms with certain existential realities or facts of life: *freedom*, which is the responsibility we bear for our decisions amid uncertain choices; *isolation,* which is the reality that no one truly understands what it is like to be us; *identity*, which is the desire to create a coherent narrative for our life story; *death,* which is the only certainty in life and the awareness of our own mortality; and *meaninglessness*, which is the dread we feel when we realize that there is no singular, objective meaning of life on which everyone can agree (Koole et al., 2006). These realities can create anxiety unless they are managed by our cultural worldview. In my view, religion is the cultural worldview best designed to address existential concerns. Put differently, religion is an ideal existential meaning system (Batson & Stocks, 2004). It's almost as if religion was designed precisely to keep our existential fears at bay. But after leaving religion, you're likely facing the daunting task of assembling a cultural worldview that addresses these concerns.

As neatly as religion checked all of the existential boxes and provided tidy answers, your new meaning system may not do so—or at least not as fully. But the problem doesn't lie with having a nonreligious worldview; plenty of people have worldviews that are nonreligious. Rather, the emotional response comes from having once had those answers and knowing what it felt like to have (nearly complete) existential security, only to have to face those existential concerns with the wisdom of having left those previous religious beliefs behind. It's knowing what you had and what you lost and living with the existential weight of that decision.

As a religious done, you are disposed to this phenomenon in a way that currently religious or never religious individuals are not; religious individuals can draw from their religious and spiritual beliefs to address existential concerns and maintain a sense of psychological equanimity in the face of threat. Never religious individuals have not previously embraced the answers offered by religion and so do not confront the same reality faced by religious dones. Rather, I think the existential chasm elicits a compound emotional state of simultaneously experiencing both grief for having lost the existentially soothing comfort offered by these former religious beliefs and the fear of having to address these concerns in new ways without the reliance on religious meaning systems or external religious authority or structures. And, depending on the religious tradition in which you were raised, it is entirely likely that you may not have fully developed the necessary skills or capabilities to wrestle with such questions given that, at least in some religious traditions or denominational expressions, relevant answers were offered in comprehensive and coherent packages, requiring only assent and memorization rather than cooperative development or internalization.

Some of you were told just to believe, rather than to challenge, doubt, or wrestle with these questions. And as a result, you may not have had practice engaging with these core fears. The result is that as a religious done, you may be at particularly high risk of existential anxiety. You might be trying to navigate the existential questions as you're still assembling a coherent and existentially satisfying meaning system. While this is in process, you might find yourself consumed with questions surrounding death, meaning, and identity. You might be increasingly afraid to die or stuck in a nihilistic state of meaninglessness. You might also find yourself wondering how exactly someone goes about answering these questions; where are reliable sources and who are trustworthy guides in this deeply personal work? And you might consistently experience the pangs of remembering what it was like to have satisfactorily quenched those existential longings through religion. Although you are no longer religious, you might long or the feelings of joy, peace, or serenity offered by religion.

So the existential chasm is both the intellectual awareness that your current answers to these existential questions are not as fully designed to ameliorate the associated anxiety or address every concern as completely, as well as the complex set of emotional responses, primarily grief over having had answers to these questions but not finding them tenable, and the fear of facing these concerns in new ways. Freedom and groundlessness are new fears as the belief in a controlling God or grand plan for the universe has eroded, leaving you feeling as though you have no guideposts for how to make decisions and bear the responsibility for your choices. Isolation becomes a concern as you realize that you are, truly, alone, and no one, or being, can really know your inner thoughts, subjective states, or lived experiences. Your identity becomes an open question because your religion is no longer a core part of your identity, nor is your religious community, relation to a divine being, or religious way of understanding the world. Death becomes a grave concern because it is the final destination, as you give up your belief in an afterlife and embrace the reality of a singular life. And you plunge into a state of meaninglessness and nihilism, asking how to make sense of this world, and your life and place in it, amid a newly revised understanding of nearly everything. You may even question life choices you've made and current decisions. In short, you may experience existential upheaval.

We each experience this ultimate dread differently. However, here are some common expressions:

- **Grief.** You might feel significant grief over the decisions you've made in the past based on your religious identity. If religion was a central part of how you structured your life, and you made high-commitment decisions based on those convictions—such as where to go to college, what to study, whom to marry, what career field to pursue—you might be lamenting those decisions now. You may also experience grief over no longer having the solace of religious beliefs and the tight-knit community of a religious group. And you might grieve having lost so much time committed to a set of beliefs or practices you no longer endorse.
- **Anger.** Many times, grief expresses as anger. You might be angry about the former decisions you've made and the consequences you're currently living with (which is an expression of the existential concern of freedom). You might also be angry with your former self for committing to religious ideals and holding on to beliefs that now feel foolish or untenable. It's also possible that you're angry at religious people, leaders, organizations, or religion in general.
- **Shame.** Sometimes, our anger hides our shame. For some, this existential confrontation brings out a source of shame in us, where we feel damaged, unworthy, or unloved. We may feel as

though there is something inherently wrong with us; part of this might be the lingering religious trauma we experienced at the hands of religious individuals or leaders. Other times, it might be feelings of shame from how we previously acted when we were religious or in the name of religion.

- **Fear.** A common reaction to the renewed confrontation with existential realities in the absence of religious beliefs is fear. These new concerns are suddenly a bit more scary—and a bit more real. Death is not easily dismissed. Meaning seems distant. Isolation feels palpable. Groundlessness is constant. And identity can be blurry and confusing. Not having the ready, certain answers of religion can feel terrifying, and you might experience considerable levels of both anxiety and depression.

Despite this panoply of negative emotions that often accompany the existential chasm, the process of engaging existential realities afresh also offers another set of concurrent responses once people can withstand the concomitant anxiety. Frequently, religious dones might report additional powerful reactions:

- **Awe.** For some, facing the existential realities without the comfort of religion can evoke awe. Feeling small, insignificant, and relatively forgettable can elicit wonder. People no longer feel beholden to a set of unreachable standards nor constrained to view the world in a particular way. They have abandoned any notion of trying to achieve cosmic significance and can, instead, be overwhelmed with the vastness of human existence. A novel sense of comfort washes over them as they see the world differently than before, and they are able to appreciate things with a new perspective.
- **Curiosity.** Some experience the chasm with a renewed sense of curiosity after leaving religion. They feel empowered to

take a fresh look at things in ways they had not considered. Many become excited about thinking of all the new ideas to entertain, experiences to participate in, and perspectives they could explore. It can feel exhilarating, like looking at the world as if for the first time.

- **Freedom.** No longer beholden to any particular set of teachings, some religious dones feel a sense of freedom they had longed for but never found. They feel unfettered by the narrow confines of a particular set of moral mandates or bound to a rigid dogma of belief. They truly feel free-floating, as if any possible future can now be theirs.

So just how do you navigate this existential chasm, and the host of negative (and positive) emotions elicited by facing ultimate realities with a newly constructed nonreligious worldview? Part of the hard work in religious change in embracing and enduring the existential distress associated with creating new frameworks for meaning. And this skill takes practice to develop.

TOWARD EXISTENTIAL DISTRESS TOLERANCE

Is it possible to learn how to face existential realities with resolution? That is, can we transcend our natural, defensive reactions to existential concerns and learn to build a strength in their wake? The Stoic philosopher Epictetus argued for this possibility:

> What is death? A scary mask. Take it off—see, it doesn't bite. Eventually, body and soul will have to separate, just as they existed separately before we were born. So why be upset if it happens now? If it isn't now, it's later. (Dobbin, 2008)

He later went on to say, perhaps more directly, "I cannot escape death, but at least I can escape the fear of it."

This sentiment captures a central part of cultivating the ability to flourish amid religious change: understanding how to develop *existential distress tolerance*. Similar to how a skill is developed through practice or fears are reduced through exposure and habituation, it's possible that we all differ in our comfort levels with existential anxiety. However, with practice and over time, it is possible that we may become more accustomed to facing existential concerns, viewing them as "truths and not threats," "facts and not fears" (Van Tongeren & Showalter Van Tongeren, 2020). Rather than seeing the existential realities as things that need to be fixed, we can learn to embrace them as inherent parts of life. We can start to increase how much distress we can face and withstand.

Some research suggests that developing a distress tolerance might be possible. For example, research on older adults offers clues: Rather than engaging in the typical defensive reactions of younger participants, older participants tend to be more prosocial and generous when reminded of their own mortality (Maxfield et al., 2007, 2014). That is, instead of responding defensively when thinking about death, older adults respond more positively and openly. Likely because older adults have more regularly encountered the existential realities of death as they contemplate their more immediate future while also losing friends and family to death, the ongoing confrontation with mortality becomes more commonplace—and perhaps they are either less distressed or better able to tolerate the concomitant stress accompanied by thinking about death. Similarly, it may be worth working to develop our own existential distress tolerance through intentional practices. But just what might that look like?

First, we need to shed the stigma of existential anxiety. Feeling uncomfortable about ultimate realities is common. In fact, feeling anxiety in general is somewhat commonplace in our current cultural climate. A good first step is not to pathologize every negative emotion or nonpositive state as problematic or pathological. It's probably

---

Learning to Tolerate Existential Distress

- Understand that existential anxiety is common. There's nothing wrong with you for feeling it.
- Accept the existential truths about life: freedom, isolation, identity, death, and meaninglessness.
- Accept that life is uncertain. We can never know what will happen in life or afterward.
- Practice distress tolerance.
- Find a support system.
- Build your new meaning system slowly, and be willing to revise.

---

rather heathy, if not evolutionarily adaptive, to feel fear when thinking about death. This fear keeps us from putting ourselves in harm's way. However, denying this fear ironically can lead us into more risky behaviors, such as flinging ourselves out of a small airplane with a parachute stuffed into a knapsack strapped to our back in the hope of proving to other people how unafraid of death we really are. When we deny our existential fears, we compensate for them in unexpected ways, which still grants them significant power over our lives. But understanding that they are simply part of life can help us not react so negatively to them.

Practically, this looks a lot like acknowledging that these fears are real, that we're not immune to experiencing anxiety around these questions, and that, at times, these feelings may be overwhelming. And when the anxiety comes, you can assure yourself it will subside. Anxiety can compound when we blame ourselves or feel shame for being anxious; rather, embracing the reality that these fears will emerge and we will find a way through can be liberating. Although it may take time, with practice, each bout will become more familiar and predictable.

Second, once we acknowledge their existence without a negative label, we can work to start accepting our existential fears. Rather than instinctively react against them or marshaling reasons for why these are misguided, how might your life change if you embraced these realities? We do have to make choices with incomplete information in an uncertain world and live with the consequences of those decisions; we are fundamentally isolated from other people, and no one will know what it is like to be you; crafting an identity that changes over time is a constant reality; everyone one of us will die one day; and meaninglessness does appear to be everywhere around us. Given these harsh realisms, how, then, will you decide to live? What will you make of your life once you become more comfortable with these difficult truths? We're able to live more authentic and fulfilling lives when we live according to our values rather than respond reactively against things that we simply don't want to be true.

In practice, this comes down to acceptance of a set of hard truths. We're often resistant to these realities because we don't want them to be true, and we had access to a worldview that seemly allowed us to treat them as if they weren't true. Instead, you can now explore them as true. Write them down and allow them to sink in. Sometimes coming to terms with these realities helps clarify our values and motivates us to cut the unimportant nonsense out of our lives. After all, life is essentially just time, and our time is limited— we should spend it wisely (Burkeman, 2021). Practice making decisions in light of these set of principles. How might your decisions be different if these realities framed your worldview?

Third, embrace uncertainty and befriend doubt. I've written elsewhere about the transformative power of humility and the benefit of knowing and owning your limitations (Van Tongeren, 2022). Although certainty feels good, none of us can know without fail what our future holds or if our own views are even correct. We would all do well to develop a deep and abiding humility about our beliefs, realizing that all of us are limited and no one holds the corner market on the truth (Haggard et al., 2018). It is normal, if not admirable, to hold doubts. It's possible that your religious upbringing discouraged doubting or shamed doubters; some may have even been told that doubting was a mark of sin or an indication that one was not committed to their faith. Ironically, it is likely those who are thinking the most about their commitments that may experience doubt. If you didn't care at all, you likely wouldn't have exerted the mental energy required to think critically about your beliefs. Doubt can be signal that you're trying to make sense of how your beliefs about how the world works fit with your experience of the world. Perhaps you can reframe doubt as an indicator that you're engaged in the hard work of sorting through your beliefs.

You might consider recalling a time when you were uncertain or didn't know something, and things turned out even better than you could have imagined. Or you can try to build your tolerance for uncertainty by getting into the habit of exploring new areas of information about which you know relatively nothing, learning something well outside your expertise, or intentionally embracing spontaneity. And when you find yourself enjoying life and finding joy, take note—sometimes uncertainty can be exhilarating and leads us to a life more enjoyable than we could have planned.

Fourth, practice is critical. Developing existential distress tolerance requires us to put in the hard work of standing in the anxiety, time and again. Considerable research has found that exposure can be a helpful remedy to certain kinds of anxiety (Hofmann & Smits, 2008). Many of us think we are unable to face distress like this. We tell ourselves that we won't make it or can't actually face these fears. But when you confront this distress head-on and come through the other side, you begin to change the associations your brain is making with these feelings of distress. You begin weakening those connections that suggest this distress is unmanageable or unbearable, and your brain (and body) starts learning that you, in fact, can metabolize this kind of existential discomfort. You are strong enough to hold these realities in tension.

Commit to taking note when you feel increased existential anxiety, as well as your first response in dealing with it. Do you instinctively grab your phone to distract yourself, change the subject to avoid the issue, pour a drink to quell the anxiety, or binge a show to numb the pain? Start paying attention to your feelings and immediate behavioral reactions. Then, when the feelings arise, pause, and feel them fully. Like a wave washing over you, they will recede, and every successive wave might be somewhat smaller—but only if you learn to experience them. Running from these fears only strengthens their potency, but practicing withstanding the discomfort will allow you to choose to respond in ways that are authentic.

Fifth, it's highly advisable to find a support system. As we've discussed, leaving religion can be an isolating experience; in some cases, many walk away from communities and relationships that have been formidable parts their lives. In other cases, leaving the faith elicits ostracism from religious community members, friends, or even family, making people feel even more alone. Identifying and connecting with a community of people who can support and accept you is crucial. What's more, it's helpful to find people who might understand the religious change you're going through. This doesn't mean you have to restrict your social circles to other religious dones (as there are pros and cons to this, which we'll cover in subsequent chapters), but it can feel validating when other people can appreciate the nuances of your experience. Disclosure builds trust and closeness, so be sure to spend time with people with whom you can share honestly and openly about your process. And for many, processing these feelings with a trained mental health clinician is another source of needed support. Practically, this looks like finding a reputable therapist and spending more time with friends and loved ones who understand you. Don't underestimate the power of social connections in helping you get through this time of adjustment.

Finally, build your new meaning system slowly—and be willing to revise. As you start to assemble a new way of answering these existential questions, your existential distress may fluctuate. Landing on tentative answers or resolutions to these concerns may provide both a small modicum of peace for having made sense of a particular pressing issue, as well as some heightened anxiety if doubts and questions swirl: What if I'm wrong? Why doesn't this feel as fulfilling? How do I know whom or what to trust? Does it even matter? Building a new worldview is a long, iterative process. You will revise, many, many times. It's rare to permanently land on a brand new worldview and adopt it, full stop. This may be a first inclination, and some people are allured by this as a potential way to shortcut the hard work of developing your own tested beliefs, but it's worth avoiding this trap. We'll unpack more about why this can be problematic in the next chapter. But understanding that for many people, their worldview is a constantly evolving set of beliefs that are revised based on the evidence of life experiences can be freeing. You don't have to get it right, let alone get it right the first time. Give yourself the freedom to get it wrong and try again.

SOLIDIFYING YOUR SOURCES OF MEANING

Religion may be one of the strongest sources of meaning, but it's not the only one. And although you might not be able to fully recreate what religion provided (e.g., literal immortality in an afterlife), a life full of rich meaning is possible. Recall the dimensions of meaning: coherence, significance, and purpose. As you rebuild after religion, here are some considerations on cultivating a flourishing and meaningful life:

- **Curiosity in assembling coherence.** The first part of meaning is making sense of the world around us. As you shift away from a religious worldview, you'll be looking for a new way to interpret the world. I can't prescribe what will appeal to you or align with your values. But I'm fairly confident that embracing curiosity as you seek a new schema for understanding the world around you is invaluable. Some people rely on science, others on secular spirituality, and some turn toward gurus or teachers to help them understand the biggest questions in the world. As you do, be aware of the lingering effects of religious residue (e.g., be careful not to replace a religious leader with another nonreligious yet still authoritarian voice telling you what to do with your life) and engage with open-mindedness and curiosity. Establish a high bar for evidence as you start reassembling a worldview that feels authentic and matches with your experiences in the world.
- **Relationships provide significance.** The second part of meaning is significance, or the feeling that we matter. As discussed earlier, relationships typically offer us one of the most enduring and memorable sources of meaning (Lambert et al., 2013). Pour into your relationships. Depending on the size and composition of your social circle, this may include making new social connections outside of your previous religious group. There are lots of ways to meet people, and the effort is worth it. Quality relationships confirm to us that we matter.
- **Establish a purpose.** The third part of meaning is purpose, or a goal that transcends ourselves. Some people find this meaning in volunteering or improving the lives of others (Van Tongeren, Green, et al., 2016). Others find it in their job, in nature, or in traveling. Research has shown that experiences are much more satisfying than material purchases (Van Boven & Gilovich, 2003). For some, travel provides awe, wonder, and gratitude,

which are all gateways to meaning (Rivera et al., 2020). Maybe you want to train your dog to be a hospice support animal. Or maybe you want to rebuild a nature trail or feed the birds in your area. The key is to do something that is larger than yourself. And it's most rewarding when such activities align with your values. That combination provides a durable sense of purpose and meaning.

APPRECIATING THE CHASM

We may never be able to fully cross the existential chasm. It may be the case that a nonreligious worldview still feels slightly unfulfilling or ill-fitting compared with one's previous religious worldview. The existential concerns may continue to sting a bit more without the salve of religious promises. But perhaps you can appreciate the chasm rather than try to leap across it. When these feelings recur, it's possible they can serve as reminders of the work you've done and continue to do. You can anchor yourself in the reality that you're living authentically, according to your experiences in life. You're crafting something new, aligned with your identity, that feels more consistent and genuine. And you're taking responsibility for it—it's fully yours. Creating meaning in the face of an uncertain future is an act of courage, and finding hope amid the chaos is a mark of bravery. With time, you may find the beauty in the struggle.

CHAPTER 6

CRAFTING A NEW IDENTITY

After walking away from religion, you'll likely be facing the task of creating a new identity. Given the pressure of religious residue and the daunting existential chasm, this can often feel like a considerable chore. During this time, you might feel rather groundless and uncertain. Where do you begin? If religion was a central part of your identity, what should direct you now? And where can you find a supportive community that understands your journey? These can be challenging questions to address, all while managing the accompanying stress that comes with a religious change. It can feel like a lot.

The goal is to develop a coherent identity driven by your values and authentic with your view of yourself. Of course, one could argue that this is a lifelong goal everyone has, and indeed they would be right—but this is a particular challenge for people who are walking away from their faith. As you assemble a new approach to life, you may be looking for new beliefs, new ways to engage with the divine or transcendent (if you so choose), new moral guidelines, and a new community. In addition, you'll be finding new answers to existential concerns. This is quite a bit to consider.

How do you do this? We'll discuss that. But before we do, we need a better understanding of the processes at play—and to discuss some tendencies you might experience along the way. Understanding more about our human nature and some strong proclivities from your religious upbringing will help you start the process of crafting a meaningful, authentic, and values-aligned identity.

EVERYONE IS "RELIGIOUS"

Let me start with a controversial claim: Everyone is religious.

If you haven't tossed this book across the room yet and you're still reading, let me unpack this. Of course, I understand that religious dones have left religion behind, and many of you would loathe to be considered religious by any conventional sense of the term. So, of course, not everyone is religious by self-designation or identity. But by religious, I mean that every person is strongly committed to their cultural worldviews as a way of understanding and interpreting the world. We may be built to believe in "religious" ways. Each of us is deeply committed to the ideological investments that help imbue our life with meaning and attempt to provide a set of answers to existential concerns. So although the content of your beliefs may no longer be religious—no longer believing in supernatural beings, attending religious gatherings, or crafting your behavior to follow a set of religious teachings—it is very likely that the psychological processes involved are very much like religion. In fact, you might hold those same beliefs just as dogmatically. Instead, now you rely on science as an explanatory framework, attend political rallies with other like-minded individuals, or orient your life and morals around a set of teachings informed by other thought leaders. If the content were different, does that sound familiar?

For those raised in strongly religious homes, this pattern feels comfortable and well-worn. You may have years of practice, indeed considerable religious residue, learning about and living out a set of ideological commitments that guide every aspect of your life. You are familiar with finding a set of ideologically similar community that affirms your beliefs (which can be quite beneficial in this case). You have plenty of experience changing your behavior to align with the mandates of an ideology or a group's norms. What this means is that as you begin to craft a new identity, one that is decidedly nonreligious in content, it may start to come together in ways that are familiar because they feel religious in process. That is, you may hold your nonreligious beliefs just as rigidly as you once held your religious ones.

I hasten to clarify that I am not saying all beliefs are equal. To be sure, the convictions based on sufficiently strong evidence are likely wholly more justified than many of those for which there is no evidence at all. Again, the content is quite different—and, in many cases, understandably, if not necessarily, so. But the style of how we hold, enact, and defend our beliefs remains rather robust. If you found yourself getting increasingly defensive as you read through the previous few paragraphs, there might be a bit of religious residue surfacing: defending our view of ourselves and the world from an antagonistic world. In fact, I would encourage you to reflect and consider ways that this residue might be affecting you even now.

Being raised religiously, especially for those whose upbringing was steeped in fundamentalism or conservative religious ideology, can lead to the maintenance of a particular pattern of belief. Your cognitive processes have been deeply etched with a specific way of holding commitments, and you will gravitate toward those when you seek new ideological frameworks. Let's take a closer look at this process.

REARRANGING PREJUDICES

A number of people who were raised in religious fundamentalist homes later find themselves leaving religion in adulthood. As we've discussed, everyone's departure from religion looks different, but many find solace in more expansive ideological worldviews after being raised so conservatively. As they shed their conservative beliefs and values, many begin to adopt new ways of seeing the world; however, how they hold these beliefs feels particularly familiar. Many people raised as religious fundamentalists leave religion but keep being fundamentalists about something else. They attach themselves to a new cause or ideology, holding it with the same zealousness and fervor as their previous religious beliefs. For some, this is politics; others find passion in a greater cause or advocacy; still others assemble a non-religious spiritual framework. The content of what people believed has changed, but the style with which they hold these beliefs remains. Here, we see additional evidence for religious residue.

This process is eloquently captured by a quote often attributed to William James (though its origins are debated), considered by some to be the founder of modern-day psychology: "A great many people think they are thinking when they are merely rearranging their prejudices."

This means that for many, the alleged act of "changing one's mind" often merely entails realigning your allegiances and altering your ingroup and outgroup. If a main driver of leaving religion was because you found religious communities to be intolerant and hateful toward minoritized or marginalized groups, and now you harbor feelings of intolerance or hatred toward religious people, James (and I) might suspect that you haven't really undergone much change: You've merely rearranged your prejudices. Changing your mind should be more than simply finding a new target for your vitriol.

The pattern of fundamentalism feels particularly comfortable for many. In fact, they may assume it's the only way to hold any belief of value or importance. So what, exactly, does it mean to be "fundamental" about a particular ideology or belief that is not religion? Researchers describe fundamentalism as a way of holding one's meaning system—it refers to interpreting all of life's events through a particular (narrow) set of ideological commitments, which provides meaning in all aspects of one's life (Hood et al., 2005). For religious fundamentalists, this usually means relying on one's holy scripture to give meaning to everything someone encounters in the world. In addition, this special meaning allows adherents to find meaning in what they perceive as an antagonistic or unsafe world. When people leave religion, they may find new (narrow) sets of commitments that shape their lens of interpreting the world and providing meaning. And they may continue to view the world, or those who oppose them, as hostile and unsafe. Often, there are implicit (or explicit) "rules" governing these beliefs, as well as how believers act. Let's unpack these.

First, fundamentalist commitments are often *puritanical*. This means that there is an expectation of ideological purity: Someone must hold all the beliefs to be a true and committed follower (Haidt, 2007; Hood et al., 2005). Any deviation from said beliefs are viewed negatively, and people gain esteem by expressing stronger or more extreme versions of their belief system. For example, if you are an advocate for addressing climate change, you may draw a significant sense of worth and identity from this commitment. You ardently recycle, volunteer to inform people about the dangers of climate change, and donate money to efforts to offset or counteract this change. You may look negatively upon people who recycle haphazardly or aren't as vocally committed as you are. And research shows that our commitments intensify when we discuss our views with other people who share our attitude about a particular issue (a phenomenon known as *group polarization*; Myers & Lamm, 1976). You must be all-in to be a true, committed advocate for climate change, or whatever your sensed mission or cause is. Purity in thought and behavior is esteemed above all.

Second, fundamental commitments often claim *epistemic exclusivity*. That means that they claim to be the only correct way to view

143

a particular issue (see Hood et al., 2005). There is no room for other perspectives to be true; they cornered the market on truth. Many religious dones shudder at the intimation that they might be holding beliefs in such a way, but take a moment and pause to reflect: Are there any beliefs (or current hot-button cultural issues or controversies) that you think you must be right about and where you absolutely would never change your mind? Start counting them. If your number of "nonnegotiables" is more than you can count on one hand (or even three fingers), you might be drawn to holding beliefs with epistemic exclusivity. It's cognitively cleaner in many regards to be convinced that you're completely right and other people are certainly wrong, but chances are you are both somewhat in error. And I realize that after reading that, you're still convinced you're at least less in error than other people with whom you disagree, but that just betrays our common human bias to downplay our own intellectual fallibilities (Pronin et al., 2002). Ask yourself, isn't it possible that you might be wrong about some of these beliefs?

Third, in groups with fundamentalist commitments, it is critical to demonstrate public allegiance to one's group. We see this frequently with people posting messages on social media or putting signs or flags in their yards or stickers on their car. It's a symbol so other people know just where you stand on a particular issue. In fact, it is often used as a barometer for true group allegiance: Do you stand in solidarity with the rest of the group, or are you timid or cowardly? Public displays of commitment are badges of honor and ways to assess who is a real group member. However, the standard always changes, and there are always new ways to show commitment and demonstrate allegiance. So it becomes a never-ending cycle of striving to meet the increasing standards of group membership. And those who don't meet these standards are castigated, publicly punished, or excommunicated; violate the group norms and suffer the consequences.

There are many instances where many of us think we are thinking, but at the end of the day, we're just rearranging our prejudices. We're moving around the good ingroup and the bad outgroup. Sure, the content is different, but the processes are the same. We haven't actually done the hard work of changing the cognitive or behavioral patterns associated with religion. We've just found something new to worship.

BREAKING THE PATTERN

The (un)holy trinity of puritanism, epistemic exclusivity, and public allegiance creates a powerful set of interlocking motivations that may shape how you find meaning after religion. These well-worn paths in your mind feel familiar and comforting—they are a form of religious residue that persists. It can be anxiety-provoking to find new ways of believing or holding your commitments. So you should be aware of some tendencies you might experience as you craft a new identity that strongly mirror a kind of fundamentalism. How can you break the pattern as you assemble a meaningful worldview after leaving religion?

- **Beware of seeking out gurus.** You may find yourself drawn to *authoritarian leaders*—people who tell you what to believe. Although these leaders may look and behave differently from leaders in your past, you still may desire for someone simply to tell you what to think and how to act (another form of religious residue). You may long for a wise sage or guru to share life hacks or disclose secret tips for finding inner peace or greater wisdom. Leaders like this are appealing because they alleviate our existential anxiety. If someone else is always telling you what to do, you never have to bear the full responsibility, or hold the weight of the anxiety, of making your own

145

choices. In the wake of leaving religion, pay attention to patterns where you seek strong leaders that give your life direction. Ask yourself whether you really align with the values they promote or if your attraction is more toward their strong style of authoritarian leadership.

- **Take caution against creating echo chambers.** You may also be tempted to repeat the pattern of *social insularity*. Here, I mean that you might surround yourself only with people who think and behave like you do. You may cut ties with people who don't hold the same commitments as you do. And while there is benefit in getting social support and being affirmed by people who see your inherent worth and value, there are also significant drawbacks to living in an echo chamber. You may lose the ability to hear different perspectives and disagree well. Your ability to navigate differences begins to atrophy because you haven't used that muscle, and it's possible that depending on your religious upbringing, you never fully developed that muscle at all. Your confidence in your own beliefs increases and capacity to withstand disagreement withers (Van Tongeren, 2022). It's a recipe for intellectual arrogance and interpersonal acrimony.

- **Avoid the allure of the "special truth."** You might also find yourself looking for a *replacement religion*. Remember the existential chasm: You recall what it was like to have a set of ideological commitments that could answer all of the existential concerns rather completely. So you might be drawn to similar alternatives or "religious-adjacent" beliefs, such as the Enneagram or astrology, which have many of the similar structures of religion without much of the religious baggage or trauma that religious dones are hoping to escape. It is worth being aware of the expectations you put on this new worldview: Do you expect this to alleviate you from the responsibility of making your own decisions or having to craft a meaningful life? Do you believe everything it says, without question? Do you think you've found a "special truth" and look down on others, with pity or disdain, who don't agree or hold your views? If so, you might have merely found a replacement religion from your original religious identity.

THE ROLE OF POLITICS

Many people raised in conservative (fundamentalist) religious homes in the United States, after leaving religion, find themselves strongly attracted to a liberal political identity (see van Mulukom et al., 2023). And the way they engage their political identity strongly resembles the fundamentalist process of their religious upbringing. The puritanical beliefs are upheld, as political polarization is rampant and political moderates are viewed as less committed, less faithful members of the group. Adherents must uphold every aspect of this ideological framework or are viewed as potential traitors or secretly conservative. An epistemic exclusivity means that people express their strong positions loudly and harshly yet are unwilling to engage in earnest, open dialogue when they disagree with others. They are reluctant, or unable, to see the merit in other perspectives or assume the goodness of the motivations of people who differ from them. And perhaps most visible of the vestige of fundamentalism is the public allegiance that results in adherents virtue signaling by demonstrating commitments through statements or actions that are publicly observable and the cancel culture that punishes anyone who is perceived to violate group norms or values even once. Purity, epistemic privilege, and devoted public allegiance sound a lot like fundamental religion but are also quite present—if not dominant— in a number of other ideological commitments, including politics. If it sounds familiar, it's because it is.

I've collected data that support this political shift after leaving religion. If leaving religion was merely about leaving politics behind, we'd expect that religious dones would report political attitudes similar to those who have never been religious. However, it may be that after people leave (conservative) religion, they rebound and become at least as liberal as, if not slightly more liberal than, say, never-religious folks (Van Tongeren et al., 2024). It's a form of *religious reactance*. Although this might appear to contradict the religious residue phenomenon we discussed earlier, the function is actually quite similar: People retain their fundamentalism as a kind of residue but have different worldview content—in this case, more liberal politics. So it is a different instantiation of religious residue in which they keep the process or personality structure but rebound in a different political content. And this is what the data say. Our cross-cultural work revealed that religious dones are at least as politically liberal as, if not slightly more politically liberal (in some cases) than, both currently religious and never-religious individuals. Indeed, after leaving religion, religious dones report being more liberal—not only more liberal than religious folks, but also some-times slightly more liberal than nonreligious folks who have never been religious before. Indeed, this suggests tentatively that after leaving religion, people may retain how they hold their ideological commitments even though the content differs.

It's important to see how this residual fundamentalism may play a role in your life because it's necessary to understand how different motives may lead you toward certain affinities as you are crafting a new identity after leaving religion. This insight can help you decide whether a particular set of beliefs is appealing because it makes sense and is consonant with your values or whether you gravitate toward an ideological commitment because it feels familiar and comforting. And it doesn't have to be politics or a religion-adjacent worldview where you end up landing. Just be aware of the strong tendency to rearrange your prejudices along the way. It's much more rewarding to do the hard work of thinking.

DUAL MOTIVES: SECURITY AND GROWTH

As you are working to craft your new identity, it's important to be aware of two fairly strong motivations that are at work. Regardless of your religious identity, when seeking to make meaning and address existential concerns, we typically face two primary motives (Pyszczynski et al., 2003). On one hand, we desire *security*; we want to feel safe, having effectively managed the concerns raised by existential questions. On the other hand, we are self-expansive and desire to *grow*; we want to learn new skills, forge new relationships, and enlarge the self. Whereas security can stagnate, growth can be unsettling. These competing motives for security and growth present themselves in different ways.

Some of my previous research has highlighted the *existential trade-offs* of *security-focused beliefs* and *growth-focused beliefs* in your meaning-making motivations (Van Tongeren, Davis, et al., 2016). Security-focused beliefs prioritize certainty, rigidity, and conviction and can offer strong answers to existential questions. These beliefs (such as the fundamentalism we discussed) provide our lives with a strong sense of meaning, permanence, and significance, and they are able to offer ready answers for the challenging questions raised by existential considerations. Intrapersonally, they are able to reduce existential anxiety and provide comfort and psychological equanimity. However, interpersonally, such beliefs are usually associated with prejudice, intolerance, and defensiveness. What this means is that you are internally settled and certain, but this certainty comes across as intolerance and dismissive of others who differ from you. Some recent research with colleagues found that rigid heaven-hell afterlife beliefs may promote prejudice and intolerance, as people view those outside of their religion as "eternal outgroups" (Reece et al., in press).

On the other hand, growth-focused beliefs prioritize questions, evolution of perspectives, and intergroup tolerance and cooperation. These beliefs assume that doubt and uncertainty are natural features of religious belief and emphasize the importance of learning from those who are different. Interpersonally, when we hold such beliefs, we are more tolerant of and cooperative with people who differ from us. Yet intrapersonally, we experience greater existential anxiety because we are tentative or hold doubts about their existentially relevant beliefs. The price to pay for open-mindedness, uncertainty, and tolerance for difference is a heaping dose of existential angst.

So the trade-offs appear to be clear: The sure safety and certainty of security-focused beliefs offer us psychological benefits but can lead to interpersonal defensiveness and intolerance, whereas the openness of growth-focused beliefs provides greater latitude to

Types of Beliefs

Security-focused beliefs	Growth-focused beliefs
• Prioritize certainty, rigidity, and conviction • Provide us with strong sense of meaning, permanence, and significance • Make us feel existentially safe • Lead to prejudice, intolerance, and defensiveness	• Prioritize questions, evolution of perspectives, and intergroup tolerance and cooperation • Do not provide strong sense of meaning, permanence, and significance • Make us feel existentially anxious • Lead to tolerance and cooperation

engage with and learn from those who are different, but at the cost of existential and psychological well-being. Because of this, particular belief systems that offer strong, compelling narratives may be attractive and might persist over time—they are able to provide their adherents with the requisite psychological and existential security. This is why such ideological commitments are so appealing. They get close to bridging the existential chasm.

The upshot of this is that as you are crafting your new identity, you should be aware of how these two motives are operating. Each of us needs to believe in something to find a sense of psychological security and resolve about these pressing existential questions. But we also desire to grow and revise our beliefs, which can be unsettling. We have to balance these two motives.

We might imagine that our desire to traverse the existential chasm is like walking across a narrow bridge. At times, you want to stop in place so you don't fall, but staying where you are due to fear doesn't allow any growth or progress. You can get stuck. But if you move too quickly or carelessly, you might slip and fall to your peril or place yourself at risk because you're lacking the requisite security and stability. Rather, it's a bit of a stop-and-go process. Many people start slowly establishing a set of beliefs that provide them with a decent amount of certainty and security—a set of tentative resolutions that address existential questions in a satisfactory way. They can hold on to these as they explore other beliefs and perspectives, knowing that they have some answers, as provisional as they may be, so they are not completely groundless. Other beliefs are fair game for revision and may change, but only after establishing a certain modicum of security first. And certainly, when life gets stressful or people feel threatened, the natural reaction is to cling to the security-providing beliefs and cease growth, at least until it feels safe enough to venture out and test new beliefs again.

THE CREEP OF MORAL SACRALIZATION

As you begin to build your ideological commitments and develop tentative answers for existential questions, be aware of the *creep of moral sacralization*. Part of creating a new set of beliefs that provides existential security is to find a set of nonnegotiables: things about which you would certainly not change your mind. This provides the requisite structure needed to offer security in the face of threat. You might imagine this as being beliefs, such as "child abuse is wrong." No one will dissuade your from your firm belief that abusing children is reprehensible. So you've committed to never changing your mind. This is a nonnegotiable belief.

That kind of ideological firmness is laudable and necessary. To a point. We need to have nonnegotiables that guide our values and anchor our moral decisions. It's essential to be committed to core moral values. But we run into trouble when we elevate nearly every issue to have the same moral status as important nonnegotiables, such as protecting children. Indeed, child abuse is wrong. But when we make every topic a sacred one, two things happen. First, we begin to dilute the truly important topics that require our moral absolutism. When you elevate your opinions about every social or political issue to the same level as the treatment of the vulnerable, it undermines the power of your care and concern for those who really deserve protection, such as children. If everything is "the most important," it comes across as if nothing is really all that important. Second, if nearly every issue is a morally sacred issue about which you are certain you are right and you will defend it no matter what, you will become closed-minded, defensive, and arrogant. You run the risk of lapsing (back) into a form of fundamentalism where you have an unflinchingly rigid set of absolute moral principles about which you are convinced you hold the moral high ground on all issues. Those who disagree are immoral or ignorant, and you will never change your mind. You've now become a religious zealot about different things.

Of course, there are topics that require moral sacredness and about which you should be certain. But only a few things. Otherwise, you'll veer into epistemic exclusivity and intellectual arrogance. Choose wisely and remain open to change your mind when you are wrong or when you encounter sufficiently strong evidence. Some things deserve our moral outrage and effort, but not everything.

BEYOND REACTANCE AGAINST RELIGION

As they begin crafting a new constellation of beliefs and coherent identity, a number of people leaving religion continue to define themselves in *reaction to religion*. That is, they take pride in being against anything religious or at all related to religion. They reflect and conclude that their religious upbringing was so terrible and traumatic that they want to do things differently. So they counteract those belief and behaviors but often do so in a reactive way. They define themselves merely as against religion.

In the short term, there are many benefits to this kind of identity formation. Indeed, many people consider being antireligious as part of their identity (e.g., Bullivant, 2022). But in the long run, a merely reactive identity can hamper your development.

Let me be clear: I think there is a time for reacting against the negative experiences some have experienced because of religious leaders, institutions, or community members. You have to metabolize and process those painful experiences, likely with the help of a trained mental health therapist and the support of a loving community. That is a normal and healthy part of the departure from religion. Breaking free often involves anger and separation from religion.

However, this process can bog down when people get stuck in ruminative patterns of being against religion. They replay their negative experiences in their own mind and in conversation with others. They find other religious dones and compare the severity of their religious histories and exit stories. Their conversations center primarily on religion and its harms. Their social groups are predominated with other religious dones whose only other point of connection of commonality is their religious past. They can "trauma bond" (although this is a bit of a misnomer, as the term really means something different) where they experience increasing closeness by sharing these hurts. But they're unable to move past this stage. It's as if even though they have left religion behind, religion still continues to define them because they're constantly pushing against it. Religion is still ruling them and how they define themselves.

Many religious dones eventually are ready to move past this stuck place. They want a fuller and richer identity.

It is critical to move from a *deficit identity* to a *presence identity*. You're not simply "not religious" or reacting against religion; you have a more complex identity than that. But as long as you continue to define yourself solely by what you're "not" or what you're against, you have forfeited your freedom to a set of religious teachings that you do not endorse and a community from which you've already walked away. In many ways, religion still is defining you.

That is why I caution against defining yourself simply in reaction against religion. You are more than that. Again, there is a time for those processes in the early stages of walking away. But just as (most) adolescents don't stay in a rebellious phase of reacting against culture as a centerpiece of their identity as they mature, so you, too, will find a richer way of understanding and living out your identity. Over time, your conceptualization of yourself will be rich with what you are and what you believe and create and how you contribute, not merely what you don't believe or with which identity you don't align. So how do you build that rich tapestry of a full and flourishing identity?

BUILDING YOUR NEW IDENTITY

Leaving religion means walking away from (some combination of) beliefs, bonding, behaviors, and belonging that shaped your previous identity. While some of you still may maintain some features religion and religious residue may linger for a considerable amount of time, building a coherent sense of self after deidentification is critical. Many of you will find yourselves assembling a cultural worldview, experiencing the world, making decisions, and connecting with others in substantively different ways. This identity (re)development process is largely a meaning-making endeavor (Bauer et al., 2008; McAdams, 2008). Each step is primarily aimed to provide us with a deeper and more authentic sense of meaning. Let's explore each component of crafting a new identity.

Build Your New Identity

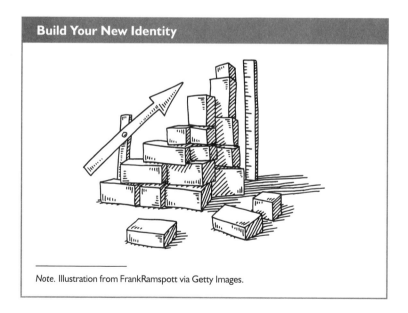

Note. Illustration from FrankRamspott via Getty Images.

Develop a New Worldview

First, religious beliefs are often replaced by *ideological commitments*. Your new cultural worldview will offer you a novel lens through which you can see and make sense of the world around you. It's a meaning-making framework that helps you understand what is happening and why. This usually comes in the form of ideological commitments that we derive from other *explanatory frameworks*— or lay theories about the world. Research sampling participants from 10 different countries around the world reveals that common postreligion ideological commitments include science, humanism, critical skepticism, natural laws, equality, kindness and caring, care for the earth, left-wing political causes, atheism, and individualism (van Mulukom et al., 2023). Although not an exhaustive list, each of these offers a useful explanatory framework for understanding the world and directing one's actions.

Given the primary role of beliefs in many religious, it can be challenging (and unnerving) to find a new set of beliefs to adopt. This process often involves trial and error—testing different commitments against your lived experience and seeing what is consistent with the evidence you gather. Some things hold up, and others do not. It may take years before you settle on a set of beliefs that feels comfortable and makes sense, and in many cases, that may also involve revising what you think or believe about religion as well. You may develop antipathy toward religion or become indifferent. Others view it as something from their past from which others may derive benefit, yet others may see it as an anathema. Or you may be very open to spirituality, as long as it is freed from traditional religion. Many people seek a nonreligious spirituality. The choice is personal. Whatever the ultimate content of your new beliefs may be, the goal of integrating a new set of ideological commitments helps offer greater meaning. It allows you to gain greater coherence

---

Common Values for Religious Dones

- Science
- Humanism
- Critical skepticism
- Natural laws
- Equality

- Kindness and caring
- Care for the earth
- Left-wing political causes
- Atheism
- Individualism

---

by helping the world make sense: It offers explanations for why things are happening. An empirically tested set of beliefs conveys meaning.

Write Your Deidentification Story

A second feature of a new identity is replacing religious bonding with an *integrated narrative*. Whereas transitioning to a religious identity is often accompanied by a "conversion testimony," deidentification does not usually have a similar ritual. There are many purposes for sharing a conversion narrative that the religious community has made a regular ritual in communal life that we could learn from, including clearly demarking a shift in who one once was (nonreligious) and who one is now (religious). It also helps highlight the ways people have changed and the power of religion in improving people's lives. In addition, it is a social ritual that publicly commemorates a private change. The convert, and all those hearing the testimony story, can point to this event as a symbolic manifestation of a shift in someone's identity. It emblazons it in the collective memory of all present and that serves powerful psychological functions. But perhaps most powerfully, the conversion testimony provides a coherent narrative for someone's life that helps shape how they, and others, view them (see McAdams, 2008). It's a statement of who someone is.

157

Write Your Deidentification Story

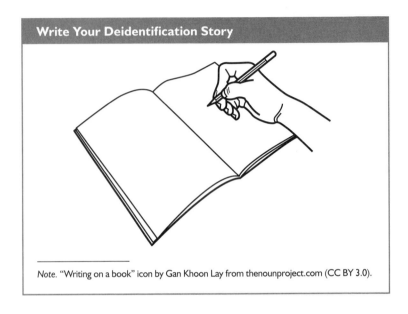

Note. "Writing on a book" icon by Gan Khoon Lay from thenounproject.com (CC BY 3.0).

The deidentification process does not have this formal ritual. To be sure, there are online communities that have invited people to share their "deconversion testimonies," and you may have found yourself explaining to others what motivated your change. But outside of these venues, you might not have had the opportunity to articulate a clear, coherent narrative about who you are now and how you got here. So you might want to take the time to write out your story of leaving religion. And if you're so bold, you could even share it with a few people you trust; doing so often solidifies our commitments (Cialdini & Goldstein, 2004). You might experience different tensions as you reflect on this writing exercise. One tendency may be to disparage your religious upbringing, and surely, depending on the nature of your religious history and the potential presence of trauma and abuse, such criticism may likely be fully warranted. Another tendency may be to view one's religious history in an overly glowing or positive light; here, too, depending on what happened and why you left, it's possible your religious history has more pain than you might be comfortable acknowledging. Indeed, when we reflect on our religious pasts, most (although not all) may recount both positive and negative aspects—parts that were hard, and parts we enjoyed. To begin to craft a coherent narrative, we have to begin with the honest truth, and this usually includes much more nuance and many more complexities than wholesale blanket evaluations. Maybe you liked your community of friends but were taught shame and fear. Or perhaps you felt the true presence of the divine but were abused by religious leaders. These complicated events elicit intricate emotions, and it can be helpful to name things as honestly as we can.

So how do you start creating an authentic, integrated narrative? Try taking a long view of your life (McAdams, 2001). If your existence is a story with many chapters, including many that have yet to be written, think of where your previous religious identity fits into this story. What were things you learned? Who were people from these chapters? And what persists now? Who is still part of your social circle? And how do you see your religious history shaping, in many different ways, your beliefs, preferences, attitudes, personality, and relationships? And how do you see your future story unfolding? Just like finding a set of ideological commitments, this process can be helpful in creating a deep and lasting sense of coherence. It can also remind you of all the ways you are significant and have a purpose. Combined, these begin to contribute to greater meaning in life.

Live According to Your Values

A third piece of your new identity is learning to move from religious-mandated moral behaviors to making *value-based decisions*. A life of authenticity and integrity is centered in living in accordance with your values. Whereas religion may have told you what was moral and immoral, for many people, leaving religion creates a vacuum in this regard. They grapple to identify clear "rules for life" as they seek how they should live. What is good and virtuous? How do I know right from wrong apart from religion? If your religion settled on many moral absolutes, you may be drawn toward views of pure relativism and subjectivity; for others, you may seek out *new absolutes* to take the place of religious teachings from the past.

As before, life is more nuanced than that. Surely a great number of philosophers have argued about morality and virtue ethics, but for most of us, we'd probably settle on a compromise that suggests there are likely some absolutes in the world (e.g., it's wrong to kill harmless people) and some relativistic or subjective decisions (e.g., the best way to help the needy or disenfranchised). Rather than looking for purely external standards to shape your behavior, many people find comfort in building an internal set of values that guide their life. What are your core values? What are your nonnegotiables, or things you would be unwilling to change or compromise? And how are you putting those values into practice in how you spend your time and resources?

As you clarify your values and begin to put into place ways to make decisions according to those values, it becomes much easier to identify a clear sense of purpose. Recall, purpose is connecting with something larger than yourself. My guess is that many of your values are oriented toward other people. As your behavior aligns with those values, your sense of self shrinks and you begin expanding beyond yourself, making deep and lasting connections. You feel less alone and more interconnected, and life feels more meaningful. In addition, your relationships will likely begin to improve, and these deeper bonds can provide you with a sense of mattering and significance. Making value-based decisions helps provide life with meaning.

Be Authentic

Finally, the goal of crafting a new identity is *authenticity*. An authentic self is one in which we are honest, secure, and consistent (Harter, 2002). We are honest about who we are, what we believe, and how we act. And critically, we accept ourselves for these very things. This acceptance provides us with a sense of security or "enoughness," where we do not feel the need to act defensively or justify our existence (Crocker & Wolfe, 2001). Out of this security, we act consistently—both within ourselves, by aligning our attitudes and behaviors, as well as with others, by being consistent in all our relationships, regardless of who we're interacting with. We don't have to hide who we are because we're honest with ourselves and secure about accepting who we are. People can observe that we act with integrity.

The pressure of religious teachings can make authenticity hard to come by. For religions that demand (near) perfection, many people may be motivated to hide aspects of themselves from others—or even themselves. Subterfuge can become standard, and we make excuses for why we can't live up to an untenable standard of holy perfection. But rather than simply own our fallibility or embrace our limitations as humans, we deny our boundedness and hide in insecurity. How freeing it is to embrace our shortcomings and accept ourselves for who we are. This freedom accompanies security, which circumvents defensiveness and allows us to present ourselves vulnerably and consistently to others. For many, walking away from religion means doing the hard, but good and necessary, work of accepting oneself and sharing that self with others. It takes replacing shame with love, fear with freedom, and striving with contentment. But it transforms relationships.

The transformative nature of authenticity allows others to see you for who you really are, rather than who you think you should be. We hide our true selves because we're afraid of rejection; if they reject a façade, they haven't really rejected us. But that keeps us from being known. The beauty of vulnerable authenticity is the possibility for deep connection and acceptance from others. They see you for who you are and love you because of it. And that is wildly and radically healing. It confirms that we matter, and that significance makes life feel incredibly meaningful.

FINDING FREEDOM

Even though crafting a new identity is often disorienting and can be scary, many find it extremely freeing. When we confront existential realities, as is required when crafting a new identity, we often must balance competing emotions. Søren Kierkegaard, a 19th-century philosopher, argued that humans are encumbered with the dual emotional experiences of awe and dread (Kierkegaard, 2005). Seeing existential realities as they are allows us to appreciate the overwhelming fullness of life, but it also gives way to be gripped by the existential angst of knowing it all will end. The existential chasm evokes fear, but crossing it brings freedom.

Awe and dread are really two sides of the same coin. We can't fully appreciate the richness of life without acknowledging we will lose it. The impermanence of life makes it so precious. Similarly, facing the fear of existential realities allows you to make authentic choices and live with freedom, knowing that you are living according to your values. Many times, people can see the world with new wonder and appreciation.

The process of building a new post-religious identity is hard, but good and long-term work. It takes time and can't be rushed. But with effort and intention, you'll begin to see that you can develop all the needed ingredients for a meaningful and flourishing life.

CHAPTER 7

NAVIGATING RELATIONSHIPS

One of the most challenging, and emotionally exhausting, parts of leaving religion is navigating relationships. Struggles abound. Some folks have mentioned that the greatest social difficulty lies in interacting with one's still-religious family and friends after walking away from faith. Relationships become strained, or broken, and many people experience the compounding grief of losing close connections with people they love. Sometimes well-meaning family members say the wrong things or simply cannot understand your choice to deidentify; other times, family members are judgmental, condescending, or downright rude about your new beliefs and identity. Some may work hard to persuade you to change, convert you back, or, perhaps even most maddeningly, assure you (and themselves) that you're merely going through a phase. They know you'll return to the fold. Episodes like this can sour holiday visits or send people packing home before the stuffing has had time cool on the Thanksgiving table.

Sometimes, it's hard to connect with old friends. At least, those friends who knew "the old you" and have a hard time coming to terms with your changes. They're not emotionally invested in seeing you change back, and they may not be judgmental or unkind, but they might not fully understand your new identity. Perhaps you used to share a religious identity and talk about religious ideas and beliefs, and now you may have less in common. You may even have a long, shared history of religious activities or been part of the same religious communities. And for some, these remnants of the past can be a reminder of a time in life they'd rather create some distance from or completely forget. So even being around them can feel uncomfortable or uneasy. In such cases, you might feel like you're losing a dear friend. In other cases, the relationship has changed and may now feel bit less deep or enriching.

Others have mentioned the challenge of finding new friends who not only understand and accept them now but can also appreciate and empathize with their religious history (and potential pain). Sometimes new friends are accepting and kind but simply cannot understand the depth or importance of your religious upbringing or the significance of your religious change. Others have mentioned the sheer difficulty of even finding new friends; where does one look, when they are accustomed to finding social connections at church, temple, mosque, small group, prayer events, or other religious settings? And once you do find friends, you might still feel different from them in important ways, given an unshared understanding of religion. It can feel isolating.

In this chapter, we'll explore how to pilot the choppy waters of relationships following religious deidentification. Usually, relationships are a wellspring of meaning; but for many religious dones, the waves feel unsettled and unsafe. We'll look to recent research that my colleagues and I conducted on how religious dones are perceived by other groups and which kind of groups they most desire to be like. We'll also see what burgeoning research on humility, and cultural humility in particular, can teach us about making social connections across deep divides. Then, we'll explore some very practical steps for reestablishing a strong community and finding relational meaning again. And we may even figure out how to make the holiday visits to the religious family members a bit more tolerable.

BETWEEN A ROCK AND A HARD PLACE

I have been deeply interested in the social lives and perceptions of religious dones. After all, research has suggested that one of the primary things that people feel is missing after they leave religion is community (Flanery, 2022). Although they experience a newfound sense of freedom, they often pay a price in their relationships. Curious as to what is behind this, I began asking questions: How do people think about those who have left religion, and what do religious dones think of religious and nonreligious people, after having left religion? These questions led my colleagues and I to conduct a series of empirical studies on the social dynamics of people leaving their faith. Sampling more than 5,000 participants, we set out to determine how religious dones are perceived by religious people and those who have never been religious, as well as which group is perceived by religious dones most favorably (Van Tongeren, DeWall, & Van Cappellen, 2023). The results were consistent and striking: Religious people prefer religious dones to never-religious individuals, whereas those who were never religious are suspicious about religious dones and do not consider them to be part of their ingroup. And the religious dones? They dislike religious people and strongly favor the never religious—a group that doesn't share their sentiment.

Why might this be? Drilling further into the data, we found that religious people think religious dones are likely to change and become religious again (Van Tongeren, DeWall, & Van Cappellen, 2023). They predict that dones are "lost sheep" that will return to the flock. But when asking dones, they confirm that they're not going back; they've left, and left for good. The never-religious individuals don't really trust religious dones. They figure that if they've ever been religious, they are

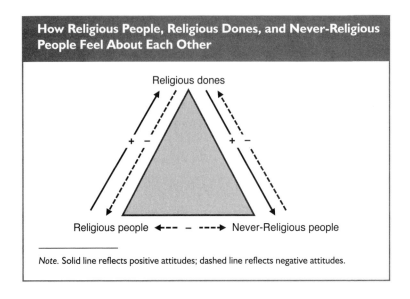

How Religious People, Religious Dones, and Never-Religious People Feel About Each Other

Religious dones

Religious people ← Never-Religious people

Note. Solid line reflects positive attitudes; dashed line reflects negative attitudes.

different in important ways. So they don't consider them to be part of their same group, despite both currently being nonreligious. They take into consideration their religious history.

The take-home message of the research is this: Religious dones are viewed by both groups as inwardly religious despite an outward nonreligious identity (Van Tongeren, DeWall, & Van Cappellen, 2023). People assume that despite saying they are nonreligious, religious dones are really still religious deep down. And because of that, religious dones are between a rock and a hard place—religious people like them and never-religious people are suspicious of them. The group they dislike and want to distance themselves from holds affinity toward them and would welcome them back, and the group they like and want to be like rejects them and mistrusts them. Because of this, and consistent with prior research, after leaving religion, you might feel a sense of loss in terms of community. In the end, this means many

Losing Your Religious Community

Note. "Refuse" icon by Adrien Coquet from thenounproject.com (CC BY 3.0).

religious dones feel isolated and alone, and data confirm this feeling is rather common.

WHY IS IT SO HARD TO GET ALONG?

Often, people wonder why it's so hard for otherwise loving and rational individuals to disagree on topics like religion. Still, it's possible that you do not view your family or certain friends as either loving or rational, in which case the answers seem much easier to come by (but which would require far more mental gymnastics). Yet many are perplexed that religion has to be a central point of contention—and likely a repeated source of conflictual conversation. Sometimes it may seem like the only thing you talk about when there are differing religious identities, especially when family is involved. Why is that?

It is possible many of you are coming from a place of love. You have a found a freedom and expansiveness and want to share that with those you love dearly. You wish the same for them that you experienced: a new way of seeing the world, a fresh perspective, more freedom, bigger ideas, broader thinking. And in turn, your friends or family members might similarly be acting out of ways that they consider to be loving: wanting you to align with their view of the world and reap the benefits they see from religious belief. It's possible that a fair amount of this struggle is motivated by what each party considers to be loving.

However, other times, it's hard to interact with friends or families because there has been significant hurt in the past. They may have said painful, offensive, or hurtful things; accused you of wrongdoing; or made assumptions about you. They may have caused significant spiritual pain or been complicit in some religious trauma you experienced. You might feel wounded. And to the degree that you want to remain in a relationship with them, you may desire for them to acknowledge the ways they have hurt you and take responsibility for the pain they caused you. For many, such confession is elusive and family members may not see that they did anything wrong.

Whether it's out of love or responding from pain, religious disagreement is thorny and difficult to navigate. Remember, religious beliefs (or disbeliefs) are cultural worldviews. They answer the big existential questions that have the potential to grip us with paralyzing terror (Pyszczynski et al., 2015). When we're sure of these beliefs, we keep this anxiety at bay (Van Tongeren, Davis, et al., 2016). However, a funny thing happens when we interact with people who believe differently from us. We get defensive and then offensive. When we encounter beliefs that contradict ours, we usually begin by defending our viewpoint. We give the long list of reasons why we're right and they're wrong, bolstering the evidentiary claims that support our position and discrediting their reasons as flimsy and their facts as misinformation or falsehoods. We remind ourselves of all the experiences we've had that reinforce our beliefs and the sheer rightness of how we see the world. I mean, what other way is there to see the world than the one, true way I see it? And even if your beliefs are tentative and doubt-filled, only an ignorant barbarian would think otherwise and hold their beliefs with certainty—of that you are certain!

After marshaling the requisite defenses to thwart the potential attack of your beliefs in the form of questioning and critique, you begin the offensive strike. In fact, you don't even need someone to outright challenge your viewpoint to move toward a posture of aggression, because, as we've reviewed before, the mere existence of alternative viewpoints suggests that one of us has to be wrong, and it's not me (Pyszczynski et al., 1999). But their presence does begin to erode our confidence. Doubt creeps in, and we begin to question the validity and veracity of our worldview. Once this happens, existential anxiety begins to make an appearance, and that anxiety can drive us to do some unsavory things. We can't manage the terror with our wishy-washy beliefs, leaving us fully exposed to the harsh realities of death and meaninglessness (and their other nasty existential friends) that our loved ones might actually point out (e.g., "Aren't you afraid of going to hell now?"). So, we go on the offensive. Anxiety can motivate anger, and we lash out in ways designed to mitigate that anxiety and get us back to a calmer baseline, like things used to be. We go after the person's beliefs, and then the person themselves if they won't change, all in the quest for our own psychological equanimity (Pyszczynski et al., 2015). We just can't make sense of their position, so we deem them as deranged or dangerous.

What does this look like when others can't make sense of our religious change? It can look like the reverse *ABCD*s (Deny, Convert, Belittle, Avoid). Let's start with D.

The Reverse ABCDs

First, people may *deny* your religious change. To the degree that they are grieving this news and their hopes for you, they may rely on denial as a reliable coping mechanism (Kübler-Ross & Kessler, 2005). Parents may especially do this as a way of preserving their expectations for a child's life or desire for their family to be religious, as they are. So they might be moving through a kind of grief. As they do, they may say you're going through a phase or discount your experiences. They may not take you seriously. Or they may point out how you are still, in fact, religious by their use of the terms. Remember, this is more about them trying to make sense of the cognitive dissonance-inducing threat your beliefs and existence now pose to them. Their worldview is being threatened, and this has more to do with them than with you. In turn, you might feel like you are explaining yourself over and over, having the same conversation ad nauseam, wondering what it will require for them to take you seriously.

After the denial efforts collapse under the weight of the reality of your consistent new identity, they may shift strategies toward *conversion*. Your beliefs may represent a threat to their cultural world-view, which can prompt efforts to change your beliefs and persuade you back to your previous religion (Vail et al., 2010). Acknowledging that you have changed, they will attempt to change you back, relying on persuasion, convincing you that you are wrong. This may be done "out of love," wanting you to see their perspective, assuming that if they just resolved a minor misunderstanding, you'd believe differently and return to religion. Or perhaps if you heard a new perspective on an issue, you'd change your mind and come back to the flock. However, as you know full well, you've thought about this. A lot. In fact, many of you have thought about this, and mainly this, for several years. You've looked at it every which way. You know it forward and backward, and by the time you've told your family and friends about your religious change, your mind was already made up. You were your own hardest critic to convince, so their pleas will likely be unsuccessful. Remember, this is again more about how you represent a threat to their cultural worldviews and their efforts to reduce their own dissonance (Vail et al., 2010). If someone they love, as smart and thoughtful as you, could change, does that mean they could, too? And if they do, what does that mean for them and how they see the world? Alternatively, does this suggest that they might be wrong? Things can unravel quickly for them.

If their attempts to change your mind are not fruitful, they may start to *belittle* you. Derogation and denigration are commonly used weapons. They may put you down and say hurtful things. Some may insult you or accuse you of unconscionable actions, making unreasonable leaps about your character based on your new identity. In short, they are othering you (Brandt & Van Tongeren, 2017). This may be the most painful part of the series of offensive reactions to your religious deidentification, especially for those who are trying mightily to maintain a relationship with your family or friends. Many people hold deep prejudices against nonreligious people, thinking that atheists are untrustworthy and immoral (Gervais et al., 2011). They may make such insinuations depending on your beliefs and what you disclose. Others may make it about them, asking how they could have failed you as a parent, when all they wanted was for their children to grow up (and stay) religious. Still others may ask personally invasive or painful questions, or simply turn to insults. As is always the case, it is important to maintain healthy boundaries. You do not have to tolerate abusive or cruel language or behavior. You have the right to state clearly how you deserve to be treated and what you will not tolerate. You can even share which topics you'd really prefer not to discuss with them. Hold your boundaries and let them know the consequences if they violate them; maybe it's ending the conversation or the visit. And then follow through if and when those lines are crossed.

Finally, many people experience that family and friends engage in *avoidance*. They create emotional and physical distance. They stop calling as regularly. Visits become less frequent or cease completely.

And when there is a conversation, it is brief and surface level. You can feel the emotional gap growing. They simply want to avoid being around you because you're a reminder of an alternative way of seeing the world, representing a threat to their cultural worldview and way of making sense of reality. If they can't change your beliefs through persuasion or shame, they'll ignore you as if you don't exist—or at least that part of you doesn't exist. That simultaneously feels incredibly isolating and infuriating. Many times, they are operating out of a place of fear and anxiety, and they genuinely may be confused about what is happening with you and what it means for them. Indeed, some recent research with colleagues found that religious dones feel less belonging in religious settings, which leads them to conceal their identity (Mackey et al., 2023). Ironically, this can create a vicious cycle: When you don't feel accepted for who you are, you hide your true self, which can lead to more isolation.

Caring for Yourself

During this time, it's incredibly important to care for yourself. After all, many of your social relationships, which are the bedrock for a meaningful and flourishing life, may be eroding or strained. They can be a source of stress and worry. So it is critical to consider ways to ensure you are caring for yourself. I see several key components of this.

- **Finding a therapist.** As I've mentioned before, finding a therapist with experience in religious and spiritual issues, especially change and trauma, can be powerful. This accomplishes a few things. First, it ensures you are carving out dedicated time to process how your religious deidentification is affecting your life in a number of domains. It sets aside this time for you to think, feel, and verbally metabolize some of these major life changes. Second, it can be so healing to have someone who cares about your well-being listen to you unfiltered. A compassionate and wise therapist can help you better understand your tendencies so you can navigate these challenging relationship dynamics with authenticity and care. Third, we often get stuck in particular ways of thinking or seeing ourselves, others, and the world around us. Having an impartial third party provide thoughtful reflection can broaden our thinking and introduce us to consider perspectives we previously hadn't. Find a licensed mental health therapist who has expertise and training in this area.

- **Shifting your social support.** A therapist is invaluable during this process, but they aren't the only people with whom it can be valuable to share honestly and openly your experience and process your feelings. Especially when desiring to process how leaving religion has changed your social relationships, this often requires finding new friends. Some people find this through online support groups or communities, and others find it in the personable interactions of getting together with others. Having a support network that accepts you and loves you is critical; it's also good to have people to do fun things with.

- **Address your physical needs.** Ensuring that you are caring for your body through rest, exercise, and good nutrition is also important. Eating healthy, drinking water, and getting sleep are always good ideas, but they are even more necessary when you're under this kind of stress. Many also find relief in exercise. Some enjoy the activity and solidarity of running, which allows them to process their thoughts and emotions while moving their bodies; others enjoy a walk with a friend or biking with a group. A restorative place for many is found in nature—be sure to take time to walk in the woods, visit the water, appreciate the birds in your area, or gaze at the stars. Nature can be calming.

- **Set and hold boundaries.** Creating and holding boundaries is really important. Be clear with yourself what you will and will not tolerate for yourself and set expectations with others about how you will be treated. Hold these boundaries firmly. This is a taxing process, and other people can make it hard because you're often disrupting their lives by not living in ways they expect you to. Some will test your boundaries, but remember to value yourself and your loved ones by not letting others treat you like a doormat. Protect your self-respect and demonstrate your dignity and worth by caring for yourself.

Reactions Toward the Reverse ABCDs

Usually, a primary response to other people's DCBA offensive is anger. This makes sense. Anger clues us into the fact that one of our boundaries has been violated (Sznycer et al., 2022). It lets us know that a value we have is not being respected by someone else. It motivates us toward action; we can use that as information to orient our behavior toward reestablishing a health boundary, voicing a need, protecting ourselves or the ones we love, and living in accordance with our values. Anger can be quite healthy. Do not try to bypass anger. Sometimes religious residue may remain, and you may feel guilty or ashamed about feeling so angry, but anger is often a necessary part of the process. If you skip over it, you'll likely get stuck and find yourself unable to move past these hurts. You can feel anger and decide how to respond, including with benevolence and kindness and/or with distance and self-protection. Again, a therapist can help you navigate this nuance and explore what is surfacing for you.

After anger, some people make it to empathy or compassion. You cannot rush straight to this step. Almost without fail, anger is a first and justifiable response. But anger, if processed and experienced, may eventually give way to compassion toward others in that you realize their reactions were more about them than they were about you (Davis, 2018). Now, let me be clear: This never justifies someone treating you poorly. You deserve respect and kindness. As my wife, Sara, a therapist, shares with her clients, this is meant as an "explanation, not an excuse." And for some, understanding this explanation can allow them to engage family and friends differently, knowing it never really was about them or their choices, but rather a reaction from a place of fear or confusion. Their whole way of seeing the world was challenged, and they're scrambling to make sense of it. Sadly, and unjustly, this may mean them reacting to you in unfair and unkind ways. Again, without justifying what they did or said, it may provide a frame of understanding—you can decide what to do with that, when you are ready, with sturdy boundaries and support.

THE FAMILY FACTOR

We've been talking about common reactions from people who are threatened by your religious change. And though I've been comingling friends and family, I want to speak directly about the complicating features that many people face when leaving religion and having a religious family. It's one thing to hear insults or experience distance from people you don't know very well, and an entirely other thing when it's people you love and thought loved you and likely played a direct role in teaching and reinforcing your previous religious beliefs. Family dynamics are much more complicated. Understanding why they are so complicated will help you better navigate the complexities of interacting with your families as you move forward.

One reason why families may have trouble with your religious change is structural. According to family systems theory, each family is an ecosystem (Broderick, 1993). This interdependent unit is best understood as an emotionally intertwined social system, replete with its own power structure and communication system. Each person has a role to play in the family, and the family has certain (unwritten) rules of operation. Religion often provides families with explicit ways to structure the family, such as patriarchal values that vaunt the father as the ultimate authority and decision-maker within a family or clear mandates for wives and children to submit and obey, often without question. As long as everyone fulfills theirs role and abides by the rules, equilibrium is maintained. Now, equilibrium doesn't mean everyone is healthy, but rather that the family system and power structure remain intact. If someone does not fulfill their role or violates one of the family rules, the family experiences disequilibrium, and there is significant pressure to conform back into the role or abide the family rules so equilibrium and proper power can be restored. If you have always fulfilled a role in your family, and leaving religion changes that role, there will be significant pressure from members of your family to get you to return to your typical role. Similarly, if a family rule centered on you (or everyone) being religious or was oriented around an explicitly religious structure, your deidentification is a blatant violation of that expectation, and you will experience significant coercion to change your behavior. Any imbalance can evoke significant emotional distress, making significant changes in a family system difficult. Typically, lasting changes require sustained efforts, wherein the family system must recalibrate to a new set of norms and roles, as it finds a revised trajectory and equilibrium. And this growth and change process can be painful.

Your leaving religion behind can send your entire family system into upheaval. When you change, the family system and structure is challenged. This is easily seen when children get married or the first grandchild arrives; families struggle to adapt to find new ways to operate as a system. Religious change can be even more significant for some families. The power differentials or perceived authority of certain family members may also be contested, as you are no longer falling in line with the wishes of those who thought they were in charge of your life decisions, especially within largely patriarchal or hierarchical systems. You're doing what you want, not what other family members, or the family unit, necessarily want for stability and balance. When you can see how your change elicits ripple effects across your family, and there will be numerous efforts aimed at getting you to fall back into the familial role and consent to the family rules, you can see how incredibly disruptive shifts like this can be for families. This doesn't mean your decision is bad or selfish or you should feel guilt for making choices that align with your values. Rather, it's an indication that family structures are difficult and slow to change, and doing so often requires weathering considerable pushback to return to the previously established status quo.

Family struggles are also more challenging because of the nature of many familial relationships. Although there are certainly individual differences and many people have had tumultuous relationships with many members of their families, there can tend to be greater feelings of warmth and connection with family members. The investment in family members is simply much greater than with many of our friends. They've been around most of our (or their) lives, and the relational histories are long. Many of us also desperately want healthy and mutual family relationships. We long for them. It's evolutionarily adaptive and normal to seek the approval and attention of your caregivers (often our parents) because for most of our lives, doing so was required to survive. We needed our parents. But as we get older, mature, and gather more resources, we are less dependent on our parents. By adulthood, many of us no longer rely on our parents for financial or practical support, but our behavioral patterns—and their views of us—haven't necessarily changed to reflect our development and maturation. We don't need them in the same ways we once did. Our autonomy is not always respected, and sometimes we don't take ownership over our own agency. Similarly, we can have strong connections with siblings, with whom we've shared formative portions of our lives and have a rich history. And many people feel a strong obligation to their family. As the saying goes, "blood is thicker than water," and many people experience a loyalty to taking care of their family. Many interdependent or collectivistic cultures more strongly value our sense of "family-self" above the individual self, which means if your cultural background is one in which group harmony and ensuring familial peace were paramount to your own decisions, family-related pressure and stress may be even more pronounced.

Surely, some people also still rely on their family to meet practical needs. Some need financial support or help with childrearing. Many deeply want their children to know their grandparents, so maintaining some form of ongoing relationship with one's parents is important, at the very least for one's children. Completely distancing from them, even if temporarily, becomes much less tenable, and their own avoidance of you is all that more painful. The relational pull to engage with and want a healthy, supportive family is natural—and part of why it's so painful when your family won't accept your religious change.

Research helps put a finer point on this. Some of my dissertation work looked at how our relationships provide us with a sense of meaning in life, and so we're motivated to repair those relationships when there is a fracture or rupture (Van Tongeren et al., 2015). I tracked more than 100 couples for 6 months and found that those who were able to forgive their romantic partner for interpersonal offenses over the course of the study reported significantly greater improvements in meaning in life from the beginning to the end of the study. Relational repair helped them not simply maintain but enhance their meaning in life. This might mean that we're motivated to repair these relationships when we sense disequilibrium or when there is a transgression, especially when existential concerns or topics are central to the disagreement (Van Tongeren, Green, et al., 2013). Doing so helps us restore the relationship and grants us meaning.

Other research has found that we're much more comfortable agreeing with people we're close to than strangers or people we don't like. That is, we strive for balance and harmony in our relationships (Heider, 1958). If we like someone, we like to agree with them; if we dislike them, we prefer to disagree with them. It's mentally simpler that way. Things get complicated and imbalanced when we like someone but cannot agree with them, or we despise someone we agree with. We can avoid this if we ignore the issue, but it's much more pronounced if the area of contention is centrally important to one of us. It also explains why once we start differing on attitudes or beliefs, we usually change our opinion of that other person. We like them less. So when our family, with whom we might have been fairly close and in agreement with on many ideas, holds a radically different view from us on something that is important, they may start liking us less, and we return the favor. We're both trying to balance our external relationships with our internal beliefs.

This process is harder with families. We're bound together, even if we don't like them. They're still our family, and we can't change that fact. So this imbalance causes us significant cognitive dissonance and emotional pain. And they are undergoing similar processes, as they try to make sense of this change from their perspective. It can make holidays stressful and phone calls anxiety-provoking. But there is hope on how to navigate these issues.

THE NECESSITY AND POWER OF HUMILITY

Besides religion and existential meaning, I've also extensively researched humility. I've been studying it for about a decade, and research has a lot to say about its value in everyday life (Van Tongeren, 2022). When it comes to navigating potentially challenging social relationships, I think humility is key. It's one place where you can put into action your desire to share the freedom and expansiveness you've found with others, as well as practice some of the inclusion that might be central to your new belief system. Let's take a look at what humility is and why it's important.

Humility has three components (Van Tongeren et al., 2019). It starts with our ability to know ourselves, which means that we accept our strengths and weaknesses, and we can own our human limitations and liabilities. Humble people admit that they are not always right, take responsibility when they're wrong, and know they haven't cornered the market on truth. It's also our ability to restrain ourselves, which looks like practicing self-control when your egoistic desires crop up. This means going beyond default selfishness, sharing the praise, and being open to differing perspectives without being defensive. And humility is also our ability to think of others and prioritize their well-being. It means that we consider how our actions will affect others, and we value their needs and welfare on par with our own. We strive to meet everyone's needs equally. Really, humility is about being the right size in any given situation: not too big and not too small.

This means that humility provides psychological security. Starting from a place where you know you are already enough allows you to admit when you're wrong (because you are more than just your ideas or beliefs), not get defensive when others disagree (because you don't need everyone to see the world the exact way you do), and be receptive to new ideas and perspectives (because you

---

Components of Humility

- Accept your strengths and weaknesses.
- Keep your ego in check.
- Consider others.

know your worth and value is constant even if your ideas or beliefs change). A truly humble person views themselves as inherently valuable apart from any idea, belief, attitude, or label—and they are free from the relentless pursuit of external approval or validation (Van Tongeren, 2022). It truly liberates them to live a life according to their values.

There are many types of humility. *Relational humility* refers to how we treat other people in relationships (Davis et al., 2011). *Intellectual humility* is concerned with ideas, beliefs, or worldviews (Davis et al., 2016). *Cultural humility* involves how we interact with people from differing cultural backgrounds (Hook et al., 2013). Although all are relevant to this topic and I strongly encourage a deep dive into this fascinating research area (Van Tongeren, 2022), let's focus now on cultural humility.

We've been talking about religion as a cultural worldview. Others have simply discussed religion as a part of culture, or a culture itself (Cohen, 2009). Indeed, you might agree that religion has its own language, norms, customs, and ways of life. You likely spent years learning it and may have thought that it was normal—even believing that everyone should think, talk, and act like that. Of course, you've long since learned that many people have different religious "cultures," including nonreligious ones. In fact, you may have experienced a kind of culture shock when transitioning from a religious to nonreligious way of life. You had to learn another culture, another language of talking about your life and the world around you. You may say that from a religious perspective, you've inhabited two cultures and can likely understand both.

Cultural humility is when we express humility around cultural differences. People who are culturally humble do not view their own perspective as superior, and they value openness and learning from the cultures of others. They especially appreciate the strength of diverse perspectives, understanding that these differences weave a beautiful tapestry of humanity. Accordingly, they listen and learn, and they demonstrate openness and respect.

> **Cultural humility:** *Expressing humility around cultural differences, including religious differences.*

I suggest that navigating social relationships with religious individuals after you have left religion requires cultural humility. In the same way that when you travel abroad, you would likely seek to understand and respect the customs of a different culture, you can learn to engage religious individuals from the perspective of their religious culture. The good news is that you already understand the language, rules, norms, customs, and rituals of religion, because it was once your cultural lens. You're quite fluent in the terms used, even if they are no longer ones that hold the same meaning to you. In fact, you've already done some of the translational work. You can see the similarities between when your religious parents tell you to "trust God," and your nonreligious friends reassure you that "the universe will work everything out." These are different cultural instantiations of similar psychological constructs. Of course, there are differences, and those differences are meaningful—in fact, those differences might represent precisely why you left religion in the first place. But you do have access to the bridge between these two cultures.

A sticking point is that it can be emotionally upsetting when loved ones or family continue to operate from a religious cultural perspective, often because it is the source of your pain. Those are often loaded terms if you've left religion, and they connote a particular set of assumptions that you disagree with or may think is downright harmful. In particular, promises of supernatural benevolence in the face of suffering (e.g., "This tragedy must have been God's will") can feel especially invalidating and distressing. And so, your reaction may be to roil against that language because it conveys a faulty assumption that you want to challenge. You simply disagree with their way of seeing the world. In fact, you know, in your very being, that they are wrong, and such views are harmful. And when you get to that point, it's likely that you've felt an impasse with your loved ones or family.

Cultural humility can help dislodge you from that stuck place. But it requires some work on your end. Now you might wonder why you have to do the work if they are ones so clearly with the problem. And truthfully, you don't have to do any work in this area. Any self-improvement around humility is completely optional. But if both parties hold firm and are unwilling to change their approach, it's highly unlikely that a different outcome will emerge spontaneously. Similarly, you could wait for them to change, but you could be waiting most of your life. Finally, you doing work around humility doesn't mean you're conceding anything, nor is it a sign of weakness. Rather, humility is a signal of strength. Given that humility requires psychological security, treating others with humility is a good sign that you're secure enough to tolerate difference and be open to other perspectives. You're not so insecure that you rely solely on the external validation of others to support the veracity of your beliefs and provide you with a sense of worth or value. You can separate your internal worth from the approval of others because you're already confident that you are enough—just as you are. If anything, doing this humility work may be marker of your own maturity and growth.

So how might cultural humility help? First, you realize that your way of seeing the world is not the only way or even the right way. Even if you are very convinced that you have improved your belief system and "upgraded" your cultural worldview, it requires you to admit that you may be wrong. After all, you've acknowledged that you've been wrong before, which is why you changed. So the chances are good that you're still wrong about something and will need to change again. Thus, you aren't the only one in sole possession of the truth and need to be open to hearing from others.

Then, you can start seeing others' responses and reactions to you through the lens of religious culture. This will help you appreciate that they are coming to their interactions with you operating from a set of assumptions. You know many of these assumptions already (having been religious), but you're open to learn about what they mean to that person and how they view you. Ask questions about what they mean and invite them to explain themselves. Be aware that defensiveness is a natural reaction, so take a moment to reflect rather than react; see what you can actually learn from what they are saying. Hear what they are trying to say, even if how they are saying it feels incongruent with your values or view of the world. You know that "I'm praying for you" and "sending positive vibes your way" are the religious and nonreligious sides to the same coin. Try to see the message (they are hoping good will come from your situation) even when the "language" differs from what you're now must accustomed to hearing.

Finally, if possible, cultural humility can help move us to empathy. Empathy can be an outward expression of your desire for expansive love. By understanding how and why people hold the beliefs they do, we can treat them with compassion and respect. We view them as equals, who are just as fully human and deserving of love and respect as we are. We resist othering them and avoid rearranging our prejudices. When we do so, we can try to move to appreciate how differences make us stronger as a community; even the religious worldviews that some people hold that you may no longer find valuable. I understand that many people think there is nothing redeeming about religion, and some people's upbringing was orchestrated in ways that only support that conclusion. I am not suggesting that you rewrite your personal history or narrative to paint it over with a positive glow or rosy outlook. That would be more damaging in the long run. And maybe there truly was nothing positive at all about your interactions with religion. But for others, it may be possible to see something redeeming about how certain aspects of other people's perspectives in this world may contribute to making it more loving, just, or kind. And if you find yourself wondering just who could believe these things, don't forget that the answer to that question is you. Or at least you in the past. You were once religious, and changed. In the way that you would want to treat your former self with compassion and kindness, you may be able to extend that same compassion and kindness to those who continue to hold the beliefs that you once did but no longer do.

PRACTICAL STEPS

I want to share some practical steps for traversing social relationships with folks who may not understand your new religious identity. This may be particularly useful when interacting with family. Each of these can help ease the complicated nature of these relationships after leaving religion.

- **Be authentic.** It's important to be yourself. I understand that this is hard. My colleagues and I found that religious dones conceal their identity in religious cultures (Mackey et al., 2023). So, too, you might strongly feel the desire to conceal your identity with your family, especially if they are strongly religious. However, over time, you'll regret it if you are not authentic. Rest assured that being yourself doesn't mean that you have to share everything. You can still hold things private, and authenticity does not require that you share verbally every thought that enters your mind. That would be ruinous for all of us. But living your new identity in a value-consistent way helps people know that you are different.

- **Set boundaries.** Any healthy relationship has boundaries. Setting boundaries is key for maintaining your own well-being. A boundary informs people how you expect to be treated and what happens if that expectation is not met. For example, a boundary could be to inform your family members that you do not want them talking about religion with your children, or you will need to end the visit. This gives clarity around what you do not want to have happen and the result if this is violated. Crucially, once you set a boundary, uphold it. If you do not, you're simply teaching other people that your boundaries can be violated without consequence and thus are meaningless. Unfortunately, this may mean inconvenience on your behalf (e.g., driving back home 4 hours and not spending the night at auntie's house because a boundary was broken), but it will establish a pattern of respect.

- **Consider who is affected.** As we've touched on, these familial relationships affect more than you. If you have a partner or children, they are likely affected by these interactions as well. Keep them in mind, and if appropriate, talk with your partner or significant other about what boundaries are needed and how this process plays out in their lives. You don't need to revert solely to caregiving, but it is valuable to acknowledge the far-reaching effects of familial or social strain on the people you love and then make value-aligned decisions from that awareness rather than reactionary responses from guilt or shame.

- **Have a support system.** This has been a resounding theme because it is so valuable. Having a supportive social community that accepts and supports you is critical, especially if your relationships with family or other friends are stressful. Because we're naturally social, we need to make sure we're meeting those needs for connection. And although, as mentioned before, we may seek out groups where we can recount our religious histories and traumas, it's valuable to go beyond this in the long run. Provide space for this, but getting stuck in a pattern of rumination can hamper growth and make you feel defined solely by your religious deidentification.

- **Know when to take a break.** Given how taxing it can be, know when to step back and take a break. Give yourself permission to skip a get-together, return a phone call further in future, or insert some relational space when things get too stressful or strained. It can just feel like too much, so knowing when to pull back before you're exhausted or depleted is important. Use that time to refocus and recharge. And when you decide to reengage, you'll be better able to make decisions that align with your values.

- **Recalibrate relational goals.** It is worth grieving that your relationships with some friends or family members may never be what they were or what you now hope for. Sometimes, people are unable to meet our needs. So it might require recalibrating your relational goals and expectations. Rather than the closeness you once shared or the feeling of approval and acceptance you long for, perhaps a more modest and reasonable target is to hope for cordial interactions where you can discuss your shared areas of common interest or reflect on positive familial memories. Being honest with yourself about what seems realistic can help take some (although not all) of the sting out of the lost relational connection.

SEEKING SOCIAL SUBLIMATION

Maybe Sartre was right, and hell really is other people. But more realistically, people are a mix of the heavenly and the hellish. Most of life's most meaningful moments involve sharing them with people we love and who care deeply about us. As inherently social creatures, we need each other. We have to embrace that those we love can be angelic some days and downright devilish others. Each of us is both flawed and beautiful, bounded by the limitations of our own humanity and trying our best from these constraints. So freedom and joy may indeed be found in the relationships we work hard to cultivate, be it your family of origin or your family of choice.

CHAPTER 8

POST-RELIGIOUS SPIRITUALITY

I started this book asserting that America is experiencing a *Great Disillusionment*. People are losing interest in participating in and identifying with a religion that no longer suits them or addresses the most pressing issues in this cultural moment. Such a claim is merely descriptive. And I've tried to explain why such an exodus is occurring and provide helpful tools for navigating the process of leaving religion. What remains less clear is what comes next. After the dust settles on this massive shift in the religious landscape of the United States, what will be the state of religion? And more importantly, what will characterize the experiences of those who have left religion?

The future religious landscape in America may look many different ways. It's possible that this disillusionment will result in atheistic secularity, with a society rooted in the morality of humanism and science as the chief explanatory framework. Or perhaps religion will simply slowly reduce its influence. It's also possible that we're actually experiencing a religious evolution that may give way to a different kind of spirituality or connection with the transcendent than what we've known so far (see Wilson, 2023). Given the possibility of persistent spirituality and the strong interest of many religious dones in remaining spiritual after having left religion, it is important to discuss different expressions of *post-religious spirituality*.

We've looked at how religious deidentification involves different features. Cognitively, it may look like moving from beliefs to disbelief. Emotionally, it may involve no longer engaging with the sacred or transcendent. Morally, it often involves no longer following the rules of religion. Socially, it can mean disaffiliating from a religious community. But there is no single path that every person leaving religion follows. And many people who no longer identify as religious still yearn for some spiritual connection. Emotionally, they still desire a relational experience with something larger than themselves. Put simply, some people who leave religion don't want to lose their "faith" in something. Remember, spirituality is the connection with something larger than oneself (that we often consider divine), so for many religious dones, the desire for spiritual connection persists. Although many people conflate religion and spirituality, these are different constructs that explain substantively different human experiences. Being done with religion doesn't mean you have to be done with spirituality. Many still desire a lasting trust in something greater than themselves or deep interactions with the transcendent. They want more.

I am not suggesting that most religious dones still want to maintain their original religious beliefs. Nor am I intimating that most religious dones are secretly harboring beliefs that make them religious. You're not a sheep in wolf's clothing. But there is a sizable number of people who, after walking away from religion, do experience longing for spiritual closeness and participation in something greater than themselves. They are looking for a post-religious spirituality that is authentic with their experiences and integrated with their values.

Some of you may not desire any spiritual connection at all. Having thoroughly disabused yourself of any supernatural belief, you may find the idea of spirituality pedantic and laughable at best and scientifically inaccurate and insulting at worst. Others of you very much desire a spiritual engagement or connection outside of the confines of traditional religion. Leaving religion did not mean that you were completely done being spiritual. Regardless of your spiritual proclivities, my hope is that you'll find this chapter useful. We'll discuss why many of us still desire some kind of spiritual longing (even if we cognitively disbelieve) and what some of those post-religious spiritualities may look like. We'll also explore alternative views to religion and spirituality, such as viewing it as an evolving quest, and a potential dark side to holding our beliefs humbly. Finally, we'll consider what any kind of faith in something larger than oneself actually means.

WHY DOES SPIRITUALITY PERSIST?

The desire for spiritual experiences persists for a number of reasons. First, as we've seen, religious residue lingers longer after people deidentify. Aspects of belief and bonding may continue even if people are finished with organized religion or no longer want to seek transcendent connection within traditional religious structures. After all, our cognitive, emotional, and behavioral patterns are well worn toward these ways of experiencing the world.

Second, people seek spiritual connection because of the existential chasm. Many may perceive a felt absence or vacuum of experiences or divine interactions that they once had. Having once experienced a union with something greater than themselves, many people may long for something more. Consciously, they may grieve no longer having formal routes toward answering some of life's deepest questions or experiencing relationships with something bigger. Drawing from work with severely or terminally ill patients, research has found that spirituality helps people address existential questions (Moadel et al., 1999). Indeed, such individuals are well aware of the reality of existential concerns and more readily draw from resources needed

191

to address their fear around these ultimate questions. Likewise, when you are facing existential questions of your own, especially after having left behind the religious answers you once held dear, spirituality may be a trusty and reliable source of comfort.

However, there is a third reason why people may continue to long for spiritual experiences after leaving religion: We're meaning-making animals. Remember that because we naturally make meaning and seek to make sense of our world, feel significant, and achieve a sense of purpose, many of us yearn for something more. Research is clear that we humans are naturally motivated to perceive our lives as meaningful (Abeyta & Routledge, 2018), and much of what we do is aimed at satisfying our need for meaning (Heine et al., 2006). Spirituality is one route toward lasting and persistent meaning that may surpass simply religious boundaries and be a natural part of many people's lives. Indeed, spiritual meaning has been positively associated with hope and negatively related to anxiety and depression, beyond the contribution of one's personality (Mascaro et al., 2004). Other work has shown that spirituality is associated with purpose among people recovering from addiction (Carroll, 1993). In fact, some of my own work has found that spiritual meaning helps buffer people from the negative effects of an adverse tragedy, such as a disaster (Haynes et al., 2017). In short, spirituality helps people sustain a sense of meaning in life, which provides mental health benefits and helps reduce the negative sequalae of suffering. And so, because people are motivated toward meaning, they continue to seek spiritual connections.

When we remember that spirituality as the perceived connection or relationship with the transcendent (Paloutzian & Park, 2014), we can see how it transcends religion. It's a relationship with something greater than yourself, and, importantly, religion is one, but not the only, vehicle for spiritual connection and meaning. When people walk away from religion, they're not giving up their need for meaning; rather, they're going to need to find new pathways toward meaning—and, for many, spirituality. For many people, leaving religion doesn't mean giving up on the spiritual. Trying to answer the deep existential questions of life (e.g., What happens after I die? What makes for a meaningful life?) often requires finding new spiritual and meaningful connections. So many people continue to seek to meet their need for meaning through spirituality, but outside of the boundaries of traditional religion. What might these post-religious spiritual pathways look like?

THE VARIETIES OF POST-RELIGIOUS SPIRITUALITY

There are several sources of spirituality. My colleagues and I surveyed more than 700 people to identify dimensions of spirituality (Davis et al., 2015). We found five sources, including *theistic spirituality*, which describes most religions: a closeness or personal connection with God or a higher being. But this was just one dimension of spirituality, and follow-up studies revealed that only roughly a quarter of participants indicated a priority for this dimension of spirituality alone. And these sources of spirituality are not mutually exclusive; people may find spiritual connection across multiple dimensions. In fact, two fifths reported an inclusive spirituality, where they endorsed all dimensions of spirituality, and nearly one fifth reported a nonreligious spirituality. (Others were low in all domains of spirituality.) Let's look at each of the other four sources.

Some might find connection in *nature spirituality*. Spending time in nature may foster a sense of closeness or connection. For example, you may enjoy walks in the woods, marveling at the stars, observing beautiful sources of natural awe (e.g., sunsets over the mountains), or communing with or caring for animals. Some turn toward astronomy, and others invest in their local parks or spend more time hiking or on the water. Many see nature conservancy and

Types of Spirituality	
Spiritual connection with	**Example behaviors**
God or higher being	Religious attendance at a temple, mosque, or church
Nature	Walking in the woods, caring for animals
Something larger, abstract, and transcendent	Contemplating our smallness and the vastness of the universe
Humanity	Appreciating human goodness and interconnectedness
Self	Living authentically and acting genuinely

pro-environmental justice efforts as spiritual activities. I experienced a deep sense of connection with something larger than myself, as well as a profound and comforting sense of smallness, when watching the Northern Lights unfold above me in Iceland and when watching the sunset while on a run between rims of the Grand Canyon.

Others might find a more *transcendent spirituality*. This describes connecting with something infinitely larger or greater that cannot be adequately described or captured by language. This may be something outside of the physical world that defies definition and is more abstract, ineffable, or overwhelming. For many of you, this might be connecting with the oneness of everything or some other force or being that evades the confines of language. Various efforts to engage the transcendent are available, including meditation or deep thought. Sometimes, we feel as though something much larger is at play, and we give ourselves over to the delight of confusion, coupled with a sense that our lack of knowledge and understanding is precisely appropriate. It can feel like an abiding peace in the largeness and complexity of the world.

Others find connection with *human spirituality*, which is the feeling of being connected with or at one with all of humanity. This may look like longing for peace, working toward justice, or feelings of deep connection when seeing humans cooperate after a tragedy. The feeling of communion when people come together to help one another or prevail triumphantly over setbacks and suffering describe human spirituality. Witnessing great acts of cooperation or human achievement may evoke feelings of closeness and connection. Many people may devote themselves toward humanitarian efforts, large or small, aimed at bettering the lives of humans around the world. Sometimes people feel this deep connection while working to rebuild after a natural disaster or when singing in unison with 60,000 other fans at a Taylor Swift concert. The boundaries between ourselves and others begin to melt, and we feel unified, connected, and much less alone.

Finally, some find their deepest spiritual connections from within. *Self spirituality* describes a sense of integrity or authenticity within oneself. Rather than being one's own object of worship, it is experienced when one has achieved a level of acceptance and acts with a degree of congruence that they feel a sense of wholeness. This spirituality arises when you feel as though you are being genuine and consistent, according to your "true self." Efforts aimed toward this kind of spirituality may include self-improvement, personal growth, and therapy.

Of course, spirituality may also look different for some. In fact, a new subfield of research is slowing burgeoning on *spiritual yearning*, or the desire for transcendent connection among those who are not religious. We may see many religion-adjacent practices that mirror aspects of religious exercises without the traditional religious structures. For example, many religious dones (especially those who have left conservative evangelical upbringings) have become increasingly fascinated with the Enneagram, which purports to be an ancient spiritual tool for understanding the archetypal nature of one's personality. Offering a supposedly complete picture of human dynamics, people are assigned (or identify with) one of nine numbers that describes their personality tendencies, including motivations during growth (healthy) and stress (unhealthy).

Certainly, it is not bad to find new sources of meaning and spiritual connection after religion. It's a natural part of being a meaning-making animal. However, I strongly recommend being thoughtful in how new worldviews are selected and followed. My therapist once wisely shared that "anything used too rigidly becomes problematic." Plug-and-replace religious-adjacent worldviews will simply swap out the content from religious to nonreligious (or "religion lite"), and you'll find yourself thinking, feeling, and behaving in the familiar patterns that led you to leave religion in the first place.

We also see this in other pursuits. Some delve into astrology to find a sense of order and significance in the chaotic world and try to make predictions about their life. Likely, this is solving the existential problem of groundlessness and freedom and the requisite responsibility that accompanies making one's own decisions. Others become strongly committed to regularly attending exercise groups, such as Cross Fit or Peloton, and find deep spiritual connection being part of a social group oriented around a larger cause or purpose—even if that purpose is one's own health and fitness (i.e., self-spirituality). This thwarts fears around isolation and identity, assuaging existential concerns.

All these spiritual yearnings address existential questions and imbue our daily interactions with the coherence, significance, and purpose needed for a meaningful life. They are new avenues aimed at closing the existential chasm and providing us with a coherent worldview. The thorny part is deciphering between what are vestiges of one's religious past and what are authentic ways toward finding meaning and answering existential questions that are value-consistent? Religious residue looms large, and we might naturally be inclined toward activities that sound, feel, and operate a lot like religion. Sometimes, people rush into these new frameworks, only later to realize they are misfitting. However, for others, these pathways lead to lasting meaning and existential comfort.

So the key is critical self-reflection and analysis. Ask yourself, do these new behaviors and perspectives align with the kind person I want to be? Do they reflect the values I want to have? Or do they just feel comfortable because they are familiar? My recommendation is that post-religious spiritual activities should be carefully weighed, selected if and when they align with your values and allow you to live a life of authenticity and integrity. Asking yourself what you value and whether a particular set of beliefs matches or does not match those values. Over time, if desired, you'll find a set of spiritual practices that help meet your deep need for meaning that feels internally consistent and value-aligned. Many desire to maintain a sense of agency in and responsibility for their life. Being thoughtful in this process will help you preserve that goal.

RELIGION AS A QUEST

Not all approaches to religion or spirituality are created equal. In fact, there is one approach to religion that is qualitatively different from many ways that people think about religious beliefs. Much closer to the "growth" end of the continuum than the "security" end, researchers call this approach *religion as a quest* (Batson & Schoenrade, 1991a, 1991b). This quest religiousness is marked by doubt more than certainty, questions more than answers, and an evolution rather than a constancy. People who identify as seeing their religion as a quest expect their religious beliefs and practices to

Religion as a Quest

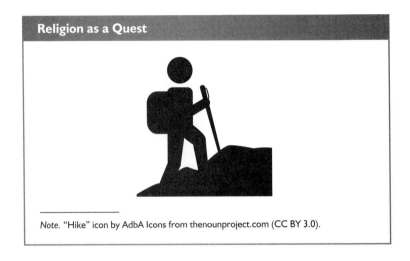

Note. "Hike" icon by AdbA Icons from thenounproject.com (CC BY 3.0).

change and grow as they change and grow. Their religious world-view is not stagnant, but rather they intentionally seek out new perspectives to expand their viewpoint. For them, religion is the journey, not the destination.

Some of you might resonate with this. You may begin to see your departure from religion as, ironically, an evolution of your religious beliefs. You may have learned enough and simply outgrown the traditional religious labels and confines of your previous religious identity. It no longer adequately describes you or your experiences and instead feels constraining and limiting. And, possibly, you may find yourself identifying with a different version of religion or spirituality in the future as you continue to evolve. This may have fueled your desire to continue to seek spiritual connection after leaving religion.

This kind of evolution maps onto previous work done on faith development. For example, one scholar suggested that one's faith develops naturally over the course of their life, moving from one stage to another, depending on developmental trajectory and ability to resolve particular questions at certain stages (Fowler & Dell, 2006). For example, this model contends that a pattern is for people to question their religious commitments in their 20s and 30s as they realize the complexities (and inconsistencies) in what they were taught. These conflicts can give way to faith maturation or departing from one's faith tradition, depending on how they are addressed. Also, people begin to be more open to different spiritual perspectives as they age, and those who stick with their faith commitments may experience a crisis of faith, where they embrace a more multidimensional view of their faith. The final stage, which is rarely achieved, is marked by a universality, where people can see the common threads of truth across religions and fully embrace and embody these teachings in their daily life and interactions with others. Similarly, you may have noticed shifts in your spiritual yearnings throughout your development.

Indeed, for many, religious views change as people do. They may move in and out of religion, or at least closer or further away. Some religious dones may begin to wonder about the role of religion for their children. Perhaps religion was a hurtful or unhelpful experience for them, but they can appreciate certain dimensions of a religious community or set of values that they want their children to be exposed to, without the other baggage of religious trauma they experienced. Others want their children to have nothing to do with religion. Still others want their children to decide for themselves what to believe, so they introduce religion as one of many options for participation. Of course, this is complicated depending on whether your child has a co-parent or you are raising children with a partner because their input will also matter greatly. Here, too, making value-aligned decisions that are consistent with your identity and beliefs is crucial.

In any case, a predominant theme in this kind of religious evolution is the centrality of doubt. People hold on loosely to what they believe, and they are open to revising these beliefs should they encounter something more convincing that persuades them to change their mind or is more squarely aligned with their experiences. Questioning and revising one's beliefs are key and distinguish this from other more security-focused religious frameworks that prioritize certainty, such as fundamentalism. And you might imagine that this is a unilaterally good thing, right? Who wouldn't want to hold their religious and spiritual beliefs loosely, when rigid dogmatism was revealed as so problematic in the first place?

A DARK SIDE OF DOUBT

My colleagues and I asked that very question: Might intellectual humility in the face of existential concerns lead to less defensiveness and greater flourishing? We reasoned that humility has generally been linked with positive responses when threatened. For example, some earlier work I conducted found that intellectual humility was related to less aggressive responses when someone criticized a person's religious beliefs (Van Tongeren, Stafford, et al., 2016). So we figured that when facing ultimate questions, such as death and meaninglessness, greater humility should likewise translate to better responses. Turns out we were wrong.

Our research uncovered a dark side of humility. Across four studies, we found that intellectual humility around existential concerns is related to poorer religious well-being (Van Tongeren, Severino, et al., 2023). In the first two studies, conducted with college students and adults from the community, greater humility around beliefs regarding the afterlife was reliably associated with greater death-related anxiety. When people admit that they might be wrong and are willing to change their beliefs around what happens after they die, they also report greater anxiety about dying. The lack of certainty that accompanies humility undermines our ability to manage existential fears.

In the third and fourth study, we found a similar pattern. Conducting a 6-week longitudinal study of college students and a yearlong longitudinal study of adult ex-evangelicals (i.e., people who left Evangelical Christianity), we found that this kind of humility predicted poorer future religious well-being. Not only did this occur 3 and 6 weeks later with college students at a religious college, but it also predicted poorer religious well-being among the religious dones sample a year later. Drilling down, we found that this loss of well-being was precisely because this kind of humility is associated with weaker beliefs about God. Over time, doubt erodes belief, which undermines well-being. There is, indeed, a dark side to doubt.

The result of this research is that those us who are prone to doubt and more open-minded to revise our deepest convictions likely are more existentially anxious and less spiritually well than those who hold strong convictions with certainty and are unwilling to change their mind. There is an intrapsychic cost that comes with being more existentially open. Now, this does not mean that humility is not worth cultivating, nor does it mean that I'm advocating for strong and certain belief frameworks, such as fundamentalism. Rather, I highlight this work to provide a clearer picture of the benefits and costs of assembling a post-religious belief structure. As you think about spiritual beliefs and practices, not only does it matter what you believe, it matters how you believe it. Humility appears to be quite good for others, but holding such beliefs humbly may incur a personal psychological cost. Knowing this can help explain what you might be experiencing when you embrace openness and doubt, as well as reduce stigma around feelings of anxiety that might arise with a newfound sense of intellectual humility.

It is possible that folks who are inclined to doubt and existential wrestling are what William James called the "sick soul." Whereas the "healthy-minded" individual finds happiness and comfort from their beliefs, which are characterized by optimism and joy, the "sick soul" feels unsettled and angsty, and their belief in the world is wrought with doubt and unease. They continually realize that what they believe about God and reality may ultimately end up being wrong. However, absent of anything else to believe, they persevere in their faith in something, until they revise and believe in something else. They have glimpsed the darkness of existential realities and know their responses to life's ultimate questions may be misguided or flatly wrong. And they carry the mental burden of this realization daily.

Maybe you are a "sick soul." In fact, I think that many people who have experienced significant adversity or suffering have been disabused of any overly positive delusions about the way life works, and instead they have a hard-fought wisdom that informs their more hardened, and realistic, outlook on life. You know the consequences of decisions and have felt the pangs of loss and grief. To be anything but burdened by these realities would be inauthentic. Many folks who have left religion—or at least even wrestled deeply with beliefs and deconstructed their worldview—resonate with being a sick soul, and they find comfort in knowing that many have found this mature approach to religion and spirituality to be an apt description. Maybe the sick souls are the ones who see the world most clearly, free from the unnecessary obligation to make everything fit into a neat, positive story.

But perhaps there is also something to learn about balancing the right amount of humility. It was Aristotle who purported that virtues have a "golden mean." Too much of any virtue is just as much a vice as too little. Perhaps in the case of humility, too much openness or willingness to revise can be ruinous; after all, you have to have some beliefs, right? Just how do you strike that balance so you don't get lost in the darkness of doubt? In addition to embracing and adjusting to the potential anxiety that accompanies openness, I see several ways forward. First, remember our dual motives for security and growth. Over the long term, we need a few firm, secure beliefs to permit greater growth. Consider what beliefs will anchor you and would require extremely strong evidence to alter. Just guard against the proliferation of these "nonnegotiables." Second, it's possible for uncertainty to be expansive; reframing a lack of knowledge as a gateway to wonder or the unknown as an invitation to curiosity and awe can help you appreciate our human finitude. Finally, requiring strong empirical evidence to change your mind can help ensure that your desire for humble open-mindedness doesn't result in a disintegrating lack of conviction. Even though you may have long abandoned any illusion of having everything make sense, you can still craft a coherent vision of the world that is consistent with your experience and brings you comfort.

FAITH AS TRUST

Finding a post-religious spiritual connection may also look different from what I've laid out. For some people, leaving religion shattered their ability to have "faith" in something larger than oneself. Indeed, *faith* is a loaded term, and many religious leaders may have misused or abused it. Perhaps you heard, "choose faith, not fear," falsely bifurcating these two concepts as bipolar ends of a spectrum. In fact, the common use of "faith," often promulgated from religious leaders and followers, now is actually closer to the opposite of faith; people often say faith to mean an unwavering commitment or set of beliefs about which they are certain. So I completely understand that many of you want nothing to do with faith.

But faith actually doesn't mean that at all. Rather, faith is probably more accurately interpreted as "trust" and certainty may engender its own drawbacks (Enns, 2019). When we think of faith as trust, we're hoping that something or someone is reliable to follow through with their commitments. For example, when we say that a romantic partner has been faithful, we usually mean it to convey that they have honored their commitment toward monogamy. Or when a someone is "acting in good faith," it usually means a decision is being made based on trust. So faith really is more similar to trust. We trust someone or something, so we have faith. We don't know for sure the outcome because no one can perfectly predict the future with absolute certainty. But the best we can do is trust based on the available evidence we have.

All of us have faith, or trust, in something. Some of us in religion, some of us in spirituality, some of us in science. Some of us trust governments or organizations and others of us people or smaller groups. Sometimes trust doesn't even require conscious thought: We demonstrate trust every time we lie in hammock (that it will support us) or board an airplane (that we will arrive alive and unharmed to our final destination), just as we trust that other drivers won't veer into our lane and cause an accident on the highway. It is likely that trust is a central part of efficient human functioning. At a certain level, because you cannot investigate everything or perfectly predict outcomes, you have to trust others.

So if you find yourself longing to believe in the spiritual after leaving religion, just know that faith or trust is a common part of human life. It makes social life efficient, and we couldn't operate in a society without certain base levels of trust. Your desire to trust and "have faith" in something is natural. And even if your faith in faith has been damaged or destroyed, it is still possible to build trust and regain a sense of hope in something beyond yourself.

RESTORING HOPE

Perhaps the strongest impetus in gravitating toward a post-religious spirituality may the desire to find a sense of hope. Spirituality may ultimately be a pathway toward hope. By this, I mean a real, honest hope, not delusion. Delusion has us believing six impossible things before breakfast and imagining all of them will come true before lunch. This delusion protects us from seeing the painful things in the world that are true and distorting them with some kind of wishful thinking where there are no consequences for our decisions and everything will somehow fix itself. This delusion is a psychological manifestation of unfulfilled fantasies of escapism that serve ego-defensive purposes to keep intact our self-esteem and overly positive view of self. We tell ourselves not to worry because someone else will fix things or someone will unexpectedly change despite overwhelming evidence to the contrary. Indeed, this was the illusion of religion that Freud described and roundly condemned nearly a century ago.

But authentic hope is different. Hope is grounded in reality. It has to be—what else could you be hopeful about if you're not clearly seeing reality as it is? Authentic hope does believe that things can be different and is an anticipation of that better reality; that anticipation should simultaneously humble us as we realize that we cannot accomplish a better reality on our own and motivate us to orient our behaviors toward making whatever (small) contribution we can to reaching that desired goal. It is courageous and bold, as well as humbling and sobering. Authentic hope reminds us that we are not the center of the world nor overly important. But we are loved, valuable, and worthy, and although we can't do everything, we can and should do something. We can make some difference. And that makes our life meaningful. Leaving religion doesn't mean you have to abandon your faith in hope.

CONCLUSION

MOVING FORWARD

Just as we can't predict the outcome of the *Great Disillusionment*, I can't predict what your future holds. Some of you have walked away from religion for good and have no interest in any intimation of the spiritual. Some of you have found ways to maintain aspects of spiritual connection and answers to existential questions apart from traditional organized religion. Others of you may have changed religions, and some of you might still be deep in the process, unsure of where you'll end up. I may be so bold to predict that some of you might, one day, find yourself slightly open to the possibility of religion again. Of course, not in the same ways as before, given the wisdom you've gained from going through this process. And this may take you completely by surprise.

In the same way, as some of you never thought you'd leave religion, I suppose that many of you think you'd never return. And you very well may be right. But some of you may have walked away for a time—years or decades, even. We humans are terrible at predicting the future but pretty resilient in living through it. One of our best qualities is that we persist. And I hope that you have seen your own strength along the way.

The deidentification process is not linear. There isn't a neat, singular path that everyone follows. Some days or months (or years), it may feel like you're stuck in a cycle or even moving backwards. Other times, you may be more confused and disheartened, overwhelmed, or just plain tired of thinking and talking about religion. Still in other moments, you might surprise yourself at how far you've come and how much you've grown. All these emotions are normal, as you seek to find a new equilibrium after leaving religion. But with time, you will experience healing and growth. It takes hope to hold on to the belief that even though you've changed, you'll find a genuine sense of flourishing again. And it may even be more free, joyful, and profound than what you've known before.

To me, a good life is one that is value-aligned, authentic, and centered on improving the well-being of others. We find deep meaning in working toward justice and expressing love. We thrive in supportive communities and when we have a broader purpose that orients our lives. For many people, religion has met these needs. But there are other avenues toward satisfying these motivations. For some, religion feels more like a hinderance than a help.

One of the core axioms guiding my work is that an honest engagement with existential realities is the only pathway toward flourishing. My hope for you is that you can honestly and bravely face the deep, existential questions of life with authenticity and resolve, accepting them as they are, and choosing to live a life of integrity. May you encounter the ultimate questions of life authentically and courageously, living a life of meaning—with or without religion.

REFERENCES

Aarts, H., & Dijksterhuis, A. (2000). Habits as knowledge structures: Automaticity in goal-directed behavior. *Journal of Personality and Social Psychology, 78*(1), 53–63. https://doi.org/10.1037/0022-3514.78.1.53

Abeyta, A. A., & Routledge, C. (2018). The need for meaning and religiosity: An individual differences approach to assessing existential needs and the relation with religious commitment, beliefs, and experiences. *Personality and Individual Differences, 123*, 6–13. https://doi.org/10.1016/j.paid.2017.10.038

Barbour, J. D. (1994). *Versions of deconversion: Autobiography and the loss of faith.* University of Virginia Press.

Batson, C. D., & Schoenrade, P. A. (1991a). Measuring religion as quest: 1) Validity concerns. *Journal for the Scientific Study of Religion, 30*(4), 416–429. https://doi.org/10.2307/1387277

Batson, C. D., & Schoenrade, P. A. (1991b). Measuring religion as quest: 2) Reliability concerns. *Journal for the Scientific Study of Religion, 30*(4), 430–447. https://doi.org/10.2307/1387278

Batson, C. D., & Stocks, E. L. (2004). Religion: Its core psychological functions. In J. Greenberg, S. Koole, & T. Pyszczynski (Eds.), *Handbook of experimental existential psychology* (pp. 145–159). Guilford Press.

Bauer, J. J., McAdams, D. P., & Pals, J. L. (2008). Narrative identity and eudaimonic well-being. *Journal of Happiness Studies, 9*(1), 81–104. https://doi.org/10.1007/s10902-006-9021-6

Baumeister, R. F., Bratslavsky, E., Finkenauer, C., & Vohs, K. D. (2001). Bad is stronger than good. *Review of General Psychology, 5*(4), 323–370. https://doi.org/10.1037/1089-2680.5.4.323

Beck, R. (2004). The function of religious belief: Defensive versus existential religion. *Journal of Psychology and Christianity*, 23(3), 208–218.

Beck, R. (2006). Defensive versus existential religion: Is religious defensiveness predictive of worldview defense? *Journal of Psychology and Theology*, 34(2), 142–152. https://doi.org/10.1177/009164710603400204

Bengtson, V. L., Silverstein, M., Putney, N. M., & Harris, S. C. (2015). Does religiousness increase with age? Age changes and generational differences over 35 years. *Journal for the Scientific Study of Religion*, 54(2), 363–379. https://doi.org/10.1111/jssr.12183

Bockrath, M. F., Pargament, K. I., Wong, S., Harriott, V. A., Pomerleau, J. M., Homolka, S. J., Chaudhary, Z. B., & Exline, J. J. (2022). Religious and spiritual struggles and their links to psychological adjustment: A meta-analysis of longitudinal studies. *Psychology of Religion and Spirituality*, 14(3), 283–299. https://doi.org/10.1037/rel0000400

Brandt, M. J., & Van Tongeren, D. R. (2017). People both high and low on religious fundamentalism are prejudiced toward dissimilar groups. *Journal of Personality and Social Psychology*, 112(1), 76–97. https://doi.org/10.1037/pspp0000076

Broderick, C. B. (1993). *Understanding family process: Basics of family systems theory*. Sage Publications.

Bullivant, S. (2022). *Nonverts: The making of ex-Christian America*. Oxford University Press. https://doi.org/10.1093/oso/9780197587447.001.0001

Burkeman, O. (2021). *Four thousand weeks: Time management for mortals*. Farrar, Straus & Giroux.

Carroll, S. (1993). Spirituality and purpose in life in alcoholism recovery. *Journal of Studies on Alcohol*, 54(3), 297–301. https://doi.org/10.15288/jsa.1993.54.297

Chen, Z. J., Streib, H., & Hood, R. (2022, November 23). *The six aspects of faith development in longitudinal analysis* [Preprint]. https://doi.org/10.31234/osf.io/akr9t

Cialdini, R. B., & Goldstein, N. J. (2004). Social influence: Compliance and conformity. *Annual Review of Psychology*, 55(1), 591–621. https://doi.org/10.1146/annurev.psych.55.090902.142015

Cohen, A. B. (2009). Many forms of culture. *American Psychologist*, 64(3), 194–204. https://doi.org/10.1037/a0015308

Crocker, J., & Wolfe, C. T. (2001). Contingencies of self-worth. *Psychological Review, 108*(3), 593–623. https://doi.org/10.1037/0033-295X. 108.3.593

Davis, D. E., Hook, J. N., Worthington, E. L., Jr., Van Tongeren, D. R., Gartner, A. L., Jennings, D. J., II, & Emmons, R. A. (2011). Relational humility: Conceptualizing and measuring humility as a personality judgment. *Journal of Personality Assessment, 93*(3), 225–234. https://doi.org/ 10.1080/00223891.2011.558871

Davis, D. E., Rice, K., Hook, J. N., Van Tongeren, D. R., DeBlaere, C., Choe, E., & Worthington, E. L., Jr. (2015). Development of the sources of spirituality scale. *Journal of Counseling Psychology, 62*(3), 503–513. https://doi.org/10.1037/cou0000082

Davis, D. E., Rice, K., McElroy, S., DeBlaere, C., Choe, E., Van Tongeren, D. R., & Hook, J. N. (2016). Distinguishing intellectual humility and general humility. *The Journal of Positive Psychology, 11*(3), 215–224. https://doi.org/10.1080/17439760.2015.1048818

Davis, J., Graham, M., & Burge, P. (2023). *The great dechurching: Who's leaving, why are they going, and what will it take to bring them back?* Zondervan. https://doi.org/10.4324/9780429493898

Davis, M. H. (2018). *Empathy: A social psychological approach.* Routledge.

DeWall, C. N., & Van Tongeren, D. R. (2022). No longer religious, but still spending money religiously: Religious rituals and community influence consumer behavior among religious dones. *International Journal for the Psychology of Religion, 32*(1), 53–70. https://doi.org/10.1080/ 10508619.2020.1871558

Dobbin, R. (2008). *Discourses and Selected Writings: Epictetus.* Penguin Classics.

Ellis, H. M., Hook, J. N., Freund, C., Kranendonk, J., Zuniga, S., Davis, D. E., & Van Tongeren, D. R. (in press). The unique associations between religious/spiritual abuse and psychological and spiritual functioning. *Spirituality in Clinical Practice.*

Ellis, H. M., Hook, J. N., Zuniga, S., Hodge, A. S., Ford, K. M., Davis, D. E., & Van Tongeren, D. R. (2022). Religious/spiritual abuse and trauma: A systematic review of the empirical literature. *Spirituality in Clinical Practice, 9*(4), 213–231. https://doi.org/10.1037/scp0000301

Enns, P. (2019). *The sin of certainty: Why God desires our trust more than our "correct" beliefs.* Hachette UK.

Exline, J. J., Pargament, K. I., Grubbs, J. B., & Yali, A. M. (2014). The Religious and Spiritual Struggles Scale: Development and initial validation. *Psychology of Religion and Spirituality, 6*(3), 208–222. https://doi.org/10.1037/a0036465

Exline, J. J., Van Tongeren, D. R., Bradley, D. F., Wilt, J. A., Stauner, N., Pargament, K. I., & DeWall, C. N. (2022). Pulling away from religion: Religious/spiritual struggles and religious disengagement among college students. *Psychology of Religion and Spirituality, 14*(3), 300–311. https://doi.org/10.1037/rel0000375

Festinger, L. (1957). *A theory of cognitive dissonance.* Stanford University Press. https://doi.org/10.1515/9781503620766

Flanery, B. (2022). I asked people why they're leaving Christianity, and here's what I heard. *Baptist News.* https://baptistnews.com/article/i-asked-people-why-theyre-leaving-christianity-and-heres-what-i-heard/

Fowler, J. W. (1981). *Stages of faith.* HarperCollins.

Fowler, J. W., & Dell, M. L. (2006). Stages of faith from infancy through adolescence: Reflections on three decades of faith development theory. In E. C. Roehlkepartain, P. E. King, L. Wagener, & P. L. Benson (Eds.), *The handbook of spiritual development in childhood and adolescence* (pp. 34–45). Sage Publications. https://doi.org/10.4135/9781412976657.n3

Gebauer, J. E., Sedikides, C., & Schrade, A. (2017). Christian self-enhancement. *Journal of Personality and Social Psychology, 113*(5), 786–809. https://doi.org/10.1037/pspp0000140

Gebauer, J. E., Wagner, J., Sedikides, C., & Neberich, W. (2013). Agency-communion and self-esteem relations are moderated by culture, religiosity, age, and sex: Evidence for the "self-centrality breeds self-enhancement" principle. *Journal of Personality, 81*(3), 261–275. https://doi.org/10.1111/j.1467-6494.2012.00807.x

George, L. S., & Park, C. L. (2016). Meaning in life as comprehension, purpose, and mattering: Toward integration and new research questions. *Review of General Psychology, 20*(3), 205–220. https://doi.org/10.1037/gpr0000077

Gervais, W. M., Shariff, A. F., & Norenzayan, A. (2011). Do you believe in atheists? Distrust is central to anti-atheist prejudice. *Journal of Personality and Social Psychology, 101*(6), 1189–1206. https://doi.org/10.1037/a0025882

Haggard, M., Rowatt, W. C., Leman, J. C., Meagher, B., Moore, C., Fergus, T., Whitcomb, D., Battaly, H., Baehr, J., & Howard-Snyder, D. (2018).

Finding middle ground between intellectual arrogance and intellectual servility: Development and assessment of the Limitations-Owning Intellectual Humility Scale. *Personality and Individual Differences*, *124*, 184–193. https://doi.org/10.1016/j.paid.2017.12.014

Haidt, J. (2007). The new synthesis in moral psychology. *Science*, *316*(5827), 998–1002. https://doi.org/10.1126/science.1137651

Harter, S. (2002). Authenticity. In C. R. Snyder & S. J. Lopez (Eds.), *Handbook of positive psychology* (pp. 382–394). Oxford University Press.

Haynes, W. C., Van Tongeren, D. R., Aten, J., Davis, E. B., Davis, D. E., Hook, J. N., Boan, D., & Johnson, T. (2017). The meaning as a buffer hypothesis: Spiritual meaning attenuates the effect of disaster-related resource loss on posttraumatic stress. *Psychology of Religion and Spirituality*, *9*(4), 446–453. https://doi.org/10.1037/rel0000098

Heider, F. (1958). *The psychology of interpersonal relations*. John Wiley & Sons. https://doi.org/10.1037/10628-000

Heine, S. J., Proulx, T., & Vohs, K. D. (2006). The meaning maintenance model: On the coherence of social motivations. *Personality and Social Psychology Review*, *10*(2), 88–110. https://doi.org/10.1207/s15327957pspr1002_1

Heintzelman, S. J., & King, L. A. (2014). (The feeling of) meaning-as-information. *Personality and Social Psychology Review*, *18*(2), 153–167. https://doi.org/10.1177/1088868313518487

Hofmann, S. G., & Smits, J. A. (2008). Cognitive-behavioral therapy for adult anxiety disorders: A meta-analysis of randomized placebo-controlled trials. *The Journal of Clinical Psychiatry*, *69*(4), 621–632. https://doi.org/10.4088/JCP.v69n0415

Hood, R. W., Hill, P. C., & Williamson, W. P. (2005). *The psychology of religious fundamentalism*. Guilford Press.

Hook, J. N., Davis, D. E., Owen, J., Worthington, E. L., Jr., & Utsey, S. O. (2013). Cultural humility: Measuring openness to culturally diverse clients. *Journal of Counseling Psychology*, *60*(3), 353–366. https://doi.org/10.1037/a0032595

Johnson, D., & VanVonderen, J. (2005). *The subtle power of spiritual abuse: Recognizing and escaping spiritual manipulation and false spiritual authority within the church*. Baker Books.

Jones, B. (2023). Reimagining Fowler's Stages of Faith: Shifting from a seven stage to a four step framework for faith development. *Journal of*

Beliefs & Values, 44(2), 159–172. https://doi.org/10.1080/13617672. 2022.2047557

Kierkegaard, S. (2005). *Fear and trembling*. Penguin Books. (Original work published 1843)

Koole, S. L., Greenberg, J., & Pyszczynski, T. (2006). Introducing science to the psychology of the soul: Experimental existential psychology. *Current Directions in Psychological Science*, 15(5), 212–216. https:// doi.org/10.1111/j.1467-8721.2006.00438.x

Kübler-Ross, E., & Kessler, D. (2005). *On grief and grieving: Finding the meaning of grief through the five stages of loss*. Simon and Schuster.

Lambert, N. M., Stillman, T. F., Hicks, J. A., Kamble, S., Baumeister, R. F., & Fincham, F. D. (2013). To belong is to matter: Sense of belonging enhances meaning in life. *Personality and Social Psychology Bulletin*, 39(11), 1418–1427. https://doi.org/10.1177/0146167213499186

Lerner, M. J., & Lerner, M. J. (1980). *The belief in a just world: A fundamental delusion*. Springer. https://doi.org/10.1007/978-1-4899-0448-5

Mackey, C. D., Van Tongeren, D. R., & Rios, K. (2023). The social pain of religious deidentification: Religious dones conceal their identity and feel less belonging in religious cultures. *Psychology of Religion and Spirituality*. Advance online publication. https://doi.org/10.1037/ rel0000502

Martela, F., & Steger, M. F. (2016). The three meanings of meaning in life: Distinguishing coherence, purpose, and significance. *The Journal of Positive Psychology*, 11(5), 531–545. https://doi.org/10.1080/17439760. 2015.1137623

Mascaro, N., Rosen, D. H., & Morey, L. C. (2004). The development, construct validity, and clinical utility of the spiritual meaning scale. *Personality and Individual Differences*, 37(4), 845–860. https://doi.org/ 10.1016/j.paid.2003.12.011

Maxfield, M., John, S., & Pyszczynski, T. (2014). A terror management perspective on the role of death-related anxiety in psychological dysfunction. *The Humanistic Psychologist*, 42(1), 35–53. https://doi.org/ 10.1080/08873267.2012.732155

Maxfield, M., Pyszczynski, T., Kluck, B., Cox, C. R., Greenberg, J., Solomon, S., & Weise, D. (2007). Age-related differences in responses to thoughts of one's own death: Mortality salience and judgments of moral transgressions. *Psychology and Aging*, 22(2), 341–353. https:// doi.org/10.1037/0882-7974.22.2.341

McAdams, D. P. (2001). The psychology of life stories. *Review of General Psychology, 5*(2), 100–122. https://doi.org/10.1037/1089-2680.5.2.100

McAdams, D. P. (2008). Personal narratives and the life story. In O. P. John, R. W. Robins, & L. A. Pervin (Eds.), *Handbook of personality: Theory and research* (3rd ed., pp. 242–262). Guilford Press.

McCrae, R. R. (1999). Mainstream personality psychology and the study of religion. *Journal of Personality, 67*(6), 1209–1218. https://doi.org/10.1111/1467-6494.00088

McIntosh, D. N. (1995). Religion-as-schema, with implications for the relation between religion and coping. *International Journal for the Psychology of Religion, 5*(1), 1–16. https://doi.org/10.1207/s15327582ijpr0501_1

McLaughlin, A. T., Van Tongeren, D. R., Teahan, K., Davis, D. E., Rice, K. G., & DeWall, C. N. (2022). Who are the religious "dones?": A cross-cultural latent profile analysis of formerly religious individuals. *Psychology of Religion and Spirituality, 14*(4), 512–524. https://doi.org/10.1037/rel0000376

Moadel, A., Morgan, C., Fatone, A., Grennan, J., Carter, J., Laruffa, G., Skummy, A., & Dutcher, J. (1999). Seeking meaning and hope: Self-reported spiritual and existential needs among an ethnically-diverse cancer patient population. *Psycho-Oncology, 8*(5), 378–385. https://doi.org/10.1002/(SICI)1099-1611(199909/10)8:5<378::AID-PON406>3.0.CO;2-A

Myers, D. G., & Lamm, H. (1976). The group polarization phenomenon. *Psychological Bulletin, 83*(4), 602–627. https://doi.org/10.1037/0033-2909.83.4.602

Newton, T., & McIntosh, D. N. (2013). Unique contributions of religion to meaning. In J. A. Hicks & C. Routledge (Eds.), *The experience of meaning in life: Classical perspectives, emerging themes, and controversies* (pp. 257–269). Springer. https://doi.org/10.1007/978-94-007-6527-6_20

Oakley, L. R. (2009). The experience of spiritual abuse within the Christian faith in the UK. (No. U500459). [Doctoral thesis, Manchester Metropolitan University]. EThOS E-Theses Online Service.

Oakley, L. R., & Kinmond, K. S. (2014). Developing safeguarding policy and practice for spiritual abuse. *The Journal of Adult Protection, 16*(2), 87–95. https://doi.org/10.1108/JAP-07-2013-0033

Paloutzian, R. F., & Park, C. L. (Eds.). (2014). *Handbook of the psychology of religion and spirituality*. Guilford Press.

Park, C. L. (2010). Making sense of the meaning literature: An integrative review of meaning making and its effects on adjustment to stressful life events. *Psychological Bulletin, 136*(2), 257–301. https://doi.org/10.1037/a0018301

Pew Research Center. (2015a). *The future of world religions: Population growth projections, 2010–2050*. https://www.pewresearch.org/religion/2015/04/02/religious-projections-2010-2050/

Pew Research Center. (2015b). *U.S. public becoming less religious*. https://www.pewresearch.org/religion/2015/11/03/u-s-public-becoming-less-religious

Pew Research Center. (2016). *Why America's nones left religion behind*. https://www.pewresearch.org/short-reads/2016/08/24/why-americas-nones-left-religion-behind/

Pew Research Center. (2022). *Modeling the future of religion in America*. https://www.pewresearch.org/religion/2022/09/13/modeling-the-future-of-religion-in-america/

Pew-Templeton. (2015). *Global religious futures project*. http://www.globalreligiousfutures.org/

Phillips, W. J., Hine, D. W., & Thorsteinsson, E. B. (2010). Implicit cognition and depression: A meta-analysis. *Clinical Psychology Review, 30*(6), 691–709. https://doi.org/10.1016/j.cpr.2010.05.002

Piaget, J. (1953). *The origin of intelligence in the child*. Routledge & Kegan Paul.

Pronin, E., Lin, D. Y., & Ross, L. (2002). The bias blind spot: Perceptions of bias in self versus others. *Personality and Social Psychology Bulletin, 28*(3), 369–381. https://doi.org/10.1177/0146167202286008

Public Religion Research Institute. (2023). *Religion and congregations in a time of social and political upheaval*. https://www.prri.org/research/religion-and-congregations-in-a-time-of-social-and-political-upheaval

Pyszczynski, T., Greenberg, J., & Goldenberg, J. L. (2003). Freedom versus fear: On the defense, growth, and expansion of the self. In M. R. Leary & J. P. Tangney (Eds.), *Handbook of self and identity* (pp. 314–343). Guilford Press.

Pyszczynski, T., Greenberg, J., & Solomon, S. (1999). A dual-process model of defense against conscious and unconscious death-related thoughts:

An extension of terror management theory. *Psychological Review*, *106*(4), 835–845. https://doi.org/10.1037/0033-295X.106.4.835

Pyszczynski, T., Solomon, S., & Greenberg, J. (2015). Thirty years of terror management theory: From genesis to revelation. In J. M. Olson & M. P. Zanna (Eds.), *Advances in experimental social psychology* (Vol. 52, pp. 1–70). Academic Press.

Reece, G., Van Tongeren, D. R., & Van Cappellen, P. (in press). Eternal outgroups: Afterlife beliefs predict prejudice. *Personality and Individual Differences*.

Reyes, N., Yu, C. H., & Lara, E. (2021). Identifying factors of deconversion from Christianity among American adults: A mixed-method approach. *Journal of Psychology and Christianity*, *40*(3), 204–223.

Rivera, G. N., Vess, M., Hicks, J. A., & Routledge, C. (2020). Awe and meaning: Elucidating complex effects of awe experiences on meaning in life. *European Journal of Social Psychology*, *50*(2), 392–405. https://doi.org/10.1002/ejsp.2604

Saroglou, V. (2010). Religiousness as a cultural adaptation of basic traits: A five-factor model perspective. *Personality and Social Psychology Review*, *14*(1), 108–125. https://doi.org/10.1177/1088868309352322

Saroglou, V. (2011). Believing, bonding, behaving, and belonging: The big four religious dimensions and cultural variation. *Journal of Cross-Cultural Psychology*, *42*(8), 1320–1340. https://doi.org/10.1177/0022022111412267

Saroglou, V. (2017). Culture, personality, and religiosity. In A. T. Church (Ed.), *The Praeger handbook of personality across cultures: Culture and characteristic adaptations* (pp. 153–184). Praeger/ABC-CLIO.

Saroglou, V. (2020). *The psychology of religion.* Routledge. https://doi.org/10.4324/9781351255967

Saroglou, V., Karim, M., & Day, J. M. (2020). Personality and values of deconverts: A function of current nonbelief or prior religious socialisation? *Mental Health, Religion & Culture*, *23*(2), 139–152. https://doi.org/10.1080/13674676.2020.1737922

Schwadel, P., Hardy, S. A., Van Tongeren; D. R., & DeWall, C. N. (2021). The values of religious nones, dones, and sacralized Americans: Links between changes in religious affiliation and Schwartz values. *Journal of Personality*, *89*(5), 867–882. https://doi.org/10.1111/jopy.12620

State of Theology. (2022). *The state of theology.* https://thestateoftheology.com

Streib, H. (2012). Deconversion. In L. R. Rambo & C. E. Farhadian (Eds.), *Oxford handbook on religious conversion* (pp. 271–296). Oxford University Press.

Streib, H. (2021). Leaving religion: Deconversion. *Current Opinion in Psychology, 40*, 139–144. https://doi.org/10.1016/j.copsyc.2020.09.007

Streib, H., Hood, R. W., Keller, B., Csöff, R. M., & Silver, C. F. (2009). *Deconversion: Qualitative and quantitative results from cross-cultural research in Germany and the United States of America* (Vol. 5). Vandenhoeck & Ruprecht. https://doi.org/10.13109/9783666604393

Stronge, S., Bulbulia, J., Davis, D. E., & Sibley, C. G. (2021). Religion and the development of character: Personality changes before and after religious conversion and deconversion. *Social Psychological & Personality Science, 12*(5), 801–811. https://doi.org/10.1177/1948550620942381

Sznycer, D., Sell, A., & Dumont, A. (2022). How anger works. *Evolution and Human Behavior, 43*(2), 122–132. https://doi.org/10.1016/j.evolhumbehav.2021.11.007

Taylor, S. E. (1983). Adjustment to threatening events: A theory of cognitive adaptation. *American Psychologist, 38*(11), 1161–1173. https://doi.org/10.1037/0003-066X.38.11.1161

Vail, K. E., III, Rothschild, Z. K., Weise, D. R., Solomon, S., Pyszczynski, T., & Greenberg, J. (2010). A terror management analysis of the psychological functions of religion. *Personality and Social Psychology Review, 14*(1), 84–94. https://doi.org/10.1177/1088868309351165

Van Boven, L., & Gilovich, T. (2003). To do or to have? That is the question. *Journal of Personality and Social Psychology, 85*(6), 1193–1202. https://doi.org/10.1037/0022-3514.85.6.1193

van Mulukom, V., Turpin, H., Haimila, R., Purzycki, B. G., Bendixen, T., Kundtová Klocová, E., Rezníček, D., Coleman, T. J., Sevinç, K., Maraldi, E., Schjoedt, U., Rutjens, B. T., & Farias, M. (2023). What do nonreligious nonbelievers believe in? Secular worldviews around the world. *Psychology of Religion and Spirituality, 15*(1), 143–156. https://doi.org/10.1037/rel0000480

Van Tongeren, D. R. (2022). *Humble: Free yourself from the traps of a narcissistic world.* The Experiment.

Van Tongeren, D. R., Brady, I., Casper, C., Fuller, H., & Swanson, C. (in press). To hell with the devil: Lingering negative religious beliefs among religious dones. *Psychology of Religion and Spirituality.*

Van Tongeren, D. R., Davis, D. E., Hook, J. N., & Johnson, K. A. (2016). Security versus growth: Existential tradeoffs of various religious perspectives. *Psychology of Religion and Spirituality, 8*(1), 77–88. https://doi.org/10.1037/rel0000050

Van Tongeren, D. R., Davis, D. E., Hook, J. N., & Witvliet, C. V. (2019). Humility. *Current Directions in Psychological Science, 28*(5), 463–468. https://doi.org/10.1177/0963721419850153

Van Tongeren, D. R., & DeWall, C. N. (2023). Disbelief, disengagement, discontinuance, and disaffiliation: An integrative framework for the study of religious deidentification. *Psychology of Religion and Spirituality, 15*(4), 515–524. https://doi.org/10.1037/rel0000434

Van Tongeren, D. R., DeWall, C. N., Chen, Z., Sibley, C. G., & Bulbulia, J. (2021). Religious residue: Cross-cultural evidence that religious psychology and behavior persist following deidentification. *Journal of Personality and Social Psychology, 120*(2), 484–503. https://doi.org/ 10.1037/pspp0000288

Van Tongeren, D. R., DeWall, C. N., Hardy, S. A., & Schwadel, P. (2021). Religious identity and morality: Evidence for religious residue and decay in moral foundations. *Personality and Social Psychology Bulletin, 47*(11), 1550–1564. https://doi.org/10.1177/0146167220970814

Van Tongeren, D. R., DeWall, C. N., & Van Cappellen, P. (2023). A sheep in wolf's clothing? Toward an understanding of the religious dones. *Journal of Experimental Psychology: General, 152*(1), 98–119. https:// doi.org/10.1037/xge0001269

Van Tongeren, D. R., & Green, J. D. (2010). Combating meaninglessness: On the automatic defense of meaning. *Personality and Social Psychology Bulletin, 36*(10), 1372–1384. https://doi.org/10.1177/ 0146167210383043

Van Tongeren, D. R., Green, J. D., Davis, D. E., Hook, J. N., & Hulsey, T. L. (2016). Prosociality enhances meaning in life. *The Journal of Positive Psychology, 11*(3), 225–236. https://doi.org/10.1080/17439760.2015. 1048814

Van Tongeren, D. R., Green, J. D., Davis, D. E., Worthington, E. L., Jr., & Reid, C. A. (2013). Till death do us part: Terror management and forgiveness in close relationships. *Personal Relationships, 20*(4), 755–768. https:// doi.org/10.1111/pere.12013

Van Tongeren, D. R., Green, J. D., Hook, J. N., Davis, D. E., Davis, J. L., & Ramos, M. (2015). Forgiveness increases meaning in life. *Social Psychological and Personality Science, 6*(1), 47–55. https://doi.org/10.1177/1948550614541298

Van Tongeren, D. R., Hardy, S., Davis, D. E., Hook, J. N., & Sibley, C. (2024). *Religious deidentification and politics* [Unpublished data, Hope College, Holland, MI].

Van Tongeren, D. R., Hardy, S. A., Taylor, E., Schwadel, P., Sibley, C., & Bulbulia, J. (in press). *Life loses meaning after leaving religion.* [Unpublished data].

Van Tongeren, D. R., Severino, M., Kojima, Y., Miskowski, K., & Blank, S. (2023). Is there a dark side to humility? Cross-sectional and longitudinal evidence for existential costs of Humility. *International Journal for the Psychology of Religion, 33*(2), 136–150. https://doi.org/10.1080/10508619.2022.2143662

Van Tongeren, D. R., & Showalter Van Tongeren, S. A. (2020). *The courage to suffer: A new clinical framework for life's greatest crises.* Templeton Foundation Press.

Van Tongeren, D. R., Stafford, J., Hook, J. N., Green, J. D., Davis, D. E., & Johnson, K. A. (2016). Humility attenuates negative attitudes and behaviors toward religious outgroup members. *The Journal of Positive Psychology, 11*, 199–208.

Wang, D. C. (2011). Two perspectives on spiritual dryness: Spiritual desertion and the dark night of the soul. *Journal of Spiritual Formation and Soul Care, 4*(1), 27–42. https://doi.org/10.1177/193979091100400103

Watkins, E. R., & Moulds, M. (2007). Revealing negative thinking in recovered major depression: A preliminary investigation. *Behaviour Research and Therapy, 45*(12), 3069–3076. https://doi.org/10.1016/j.brat.2007.05.001

Wilson, R. (2023). *Soul boom: Why we need a spiritual revolution.* Hatchette Book Group.

Wright, B. R., Giovanelli, D., Dolan, E. G., & Edwards, M. E. (2011). Explaining deconversion from Christianity: A study of online narratives. *Journal of Religion and Society, 13*, 1–17.

INDEX

Abuse, 38, 40, 49
Accommodation, 32–33
Adherence to behavioral mandates,
    discontinuation of, 68, 71–72
Adversity, remaking meaning after,
    108–109
Affiliation, religious, 4, 11
Agnosticism, 5
Agreeableness, as predictor of leaving,
    40–41
Allegiance, public, 144, 147
American Evangelicalism, 26
Anger, 128, 174
Antipathy, 74–77
Aristotle, 202
Assimilation, 32
Atheism, 5
Atheistic secularity, 189
Attitudes, persistence of religious, 88–89
Authentic hope, 205
Authenticity, 161–162, 185
Authoritarian leaders, 145–146
Avoidance, 171–172
Awareness, conscious, 89–90
Awe, 129, 162

Behavioral changes, 104
Behavioral mandates, discontinuation
    of adherence to, 68, 71–72

Behaviors, 89, 94
Belief(s)
    examination of, 42
    in God, lack of, 68–70
    growth/security-focused, 149–151,
        203
    negative religious, 95–96
    non-negotiable, 152–153
    "religion-adjacent," 146
Belittling, 171
Belonging, desire for, 112, 115–117
"Bloody Mary," 93–94
Boundaries, 171, 174, 186
Breaking patterns, 145–147

Catholic Church, 24
Certainty, desire for, 112–115
Changes after leaving religion, 74–80
Chasm, existential. See Existential
    chasm
Childhelp National Child Abuse
    Hotline, 56
Christianity, 3–4, 11, 29, 30
Closure, desire for, 112–115
Cognitive dissonance, 42, 170–171
Cognitive prioritization of negative
    information, 96–97
Coherence, 109
Comfort, 42–43

Commitments, ideological, 156
Communities, 57, 100, 115–117, 135,
    165–166, 173
Compassion, 174
Connection, transcendent, 120
Conscientiousness, as predictor of
    leaving, 40
Conscious awareness, 89–90
Consumer behavior, 92
Control, illusions of, 113
Conversion, 170–171
COVID pandemic, 113
Creep of moral sacrilization, 152–153
Criticism, moral, 71
Cultural humility, 181–185
Cultural stagnation, 20–24
Cultural worldviews, 119–121, 172
Curiosity, 129–130, 137

Dark side of doubt, 200–203
Darker side of religion, 93–97
DCBAs. See Reverse ABCDs
Death, 125, 128
Decisions, value-based, 159–160
Deconstruction, 7, 28, 61–67, 82
Deconversion, emotional suffering
    phase of, 70
De-emphasis, 74–76
Defensiveness, strategic, 107
Deficit identity, 154
Deidentification, 7, 66–73, 157–159
Denial, 68–70, 169–170
Devil, 93–94
Disaffiliates, 79
Disagreements, 168
Disbelief in God, 68–70
Disbelievers, 78–79
Disclosure, 135
Discontinuation of adherence to
    behavioral mandates, 68, 71–72
Discontinued dones, 73–74
Discontinuers, 79
Disengagers, 79
Dissonance, cognitive, 42, 170–171

Distinct departures, 73–74
Distress tolerance, existential, 130–136
Divine struggles, 65
Dones, 4, 74
Doubt, 62–63, 133, 134, 200–203
Dread, 162

Egos, 180
Emotional disengagement, from God,
    68, 70–71
Emotional variability, as predictor of
    leaving, 40–41
Emotions, religious, persistence of, 89
Empathy, 174
Enneagram, 77, 196
Epictetus, 130
Epistemic exclusivity, 143–144, 147
"Eternal outgroups," 150
Evangelicalism, 26, 29, 30, 36, 90
Examination of beliefs, 42
Exclusivity, epistemic, 143–144
Existential chasm, 125–130, 138, 191
Existential distress tolerance, 130–136
Existential trade-offs, 149
Exline, J. J., 65
Explanatory frameworks, 156

Faith as trust, 203–204
Falwell, Jerry, 105–106
Family dynamics, 175, 186
Family systems theory, 175–179
Fear, 129
Four horsemen of religion's apocalypse,
    19–37
    commonalities of, 31–35
    cultural stagnation, 20–24
    the problematic label, 20–21, 29–31
    recent support for, 35–37
    religious trauma, 20–21, 24–26
    simplistic views of suffering, 20–21,
        26–29
Fowler, J. W., 81
Frameworks, explanatory, 156
Freedom, 125, 130, 162

Freud, S., 3, 205
Fundamentalism, 142, 147, 148, 152
The Future of an Illusion (Freud), 3
Future religious landscape, 189

Great Disillusionment, 3–4, 6, 36, 189
Grief, 128
Group polarization, 143
Growth-focused beliefs, 149–151, 203
Gurus, 145–146

Habits, 98–99
Harris, Joshua, 17–18
Hell, 94
Hope, 204–205
Human spirituality, 194–195
Humility, 133, 179–185, 200–202

Identity, 125, 154
    deficit, 154
    deidentification, 7, 66–73, 157–159
    liberal political, 147
    new identities. *See* New identities
    presence, 154
Ideological commitments, 156
I Kissed Dating Goodbye (Harris), 17
Illusory pattern recognition, 94
Immortality, symbolic, 117–118
Inclusive spirituality, 193
Insularity, social, 146
Integrated narrative, 157
Intellectual denial, 68–70
Intellectual humility, 181
Interpersonal struggles, 65
Intolerance, 23
Intrapersonal struggles, 65
Islam, 3
Isolation, 125

James, William, 142, 201
Jesus, 30
Just world, 27

Kierkegaard, Søren, 162

Label, problematic, 20–21, 29–31, 34
Leaders, authoritarian, 145–146
Leaving, 38–41
LGBTQ+ individuals, 19, 23, 24, 49
Liberal political identity, 147
Loss, remaking meaning after, 108–109

Meaning in life, 105–134
    cultural worldviews, 119–121, 172
    and existential chasm, 125–130,
        138, 191
    and existential distress tolerance,
        130–136
    human need for, 106–108
    loss of, 121–125
    origins of, 111–118
    remaking after adversity/loss,
        108–109
    sources of, 136–138
    as term, 108–110
Meaninglessness, 125
Meaning maintenance model, 111
Meaning-making, 192
Men, 40
Minorities, racial and ethnic, 23
Mistrust of science, 23
Moral criticism, 71
Morals, 91
Moral sacralization, 152–153

Narcissism, spiritual, 53–55
Narrative, integrated, 157
National Sexual Assault Hotline, 56
Nature spirituality, 193–194
Negative religious beliefs, 95–96
Neuroticism, as predictor of leaving,
    40
New experiences, as predictor of
    leaving, 40
New identities, 139–162
    and authenticity, 161–162
    and breaking the patterns, 145–147
    and creep of moral sacralization,
        152–153

New identities *(continued)*
and deidentification story, 157–159
and freedom, 162
and new worldviews, 156–157
and prejudices, 141–145
and reactions to religion, 153–154
and role of politics, 147–149
and security and growth, 149–151
and value-based decisions, 159–160
Nihilism, 123–125
Nones, 4, 7, 11–12
Nonreligious spirituality, 193

Online resources, 57
Openness to new experiences,
as predictor of leaving, 40
Othering, 171
Outgroups, eternal, 150

Patriarchy, 23
Pattern recognition, illusory, 94
Patterns, breaking, 145–147
Persistence of spirituality, 191–193
Personality features, as predictor of
leaving, 40
Pew Research Center, 3–4, 30
Physical needs, 173
Polarization, group, 143
Political identity, liberal, 147
Politics, role of, 147–149
Postreligious spirituality, 189–205
and the dark side of doubt, 200–203
and faith as trust, 203–204
persistence of spirituality, 191–193
religion as quest, 197–200
and restoring hope, 204–205
varieties of, 193–197
Practice, in confronting distress,
134–135
Predictors, of leaving, 38–41
Prejudices, 141–145
Presence identity, 154
Problematic label, 20–21, 29–31, 34
Problem of evil, 27

Prosocial behaviors, persistence of, 89
Prosperity gospel, 26
Protestant Evangelicalism, 90
Pro-Trump Republicanism, 36
Psychological vulnerability, 49
Public allegiance, 144, 147
Puritanicalism, 143
Purity, 17, 23, 72, 143, 147
Purpose, sense of, 109–110, 137–138,
160

Questioning, 63–64

Racial and ethnic minorities, 23
Reactions to religion, 153–154
Reasons for leaving, reflection on, 41
Reconstruction, 7, 36, 66–67, 80–81
Reflection on reasons for leaving, 41
Relational goals, 187
Relational humility, 181
Relational repair, 178
Relationships, 137, 163–188
desire for, 112, 115–117
difficulties with, 167–169
and humility, 179–185
perceptions of, 165–167
practical steps for, 185–187
reverse ABCDs, 169–172, 174–185
and self-care, 172–174
Religion
changes after leaving, 74–80
darker side of, 93–97
as quest, 197–200
reactions to, 153–154
and replacement "religion," 146
role of, for children, 199
sprawling effect of, 91–93
walking away from. *See* Walking
away from religion
Religion-adjacent beliefs, 146
Religious affiliation, 4, 11
Religious attitudes, persistence of,
88–89
Religious behaviors, persistence of, 89

Religious communities, 100, 115–117
Religious disagreements, 168
Religious emotions, persistence of, 89
Religious families, 175
Religious groups, with history of
   abuse, 49
Religious history, 87–88
Religiously unaffiliated. *See* Nones
Religious reactance, 148
Religious residue, 12, 85–104, 191
   darker side of religion, 93–97
   living with, 101–104
   nature of, 86–91
   persistence of, 97–101
   sprawling effect of religion, 91–93
Religious trauma, 20–21, 24–26, 45–58
   and cascading erosion of trust,
      50–53
   coping with, 55–58
   effects of, 49–50
   and spiritual narcissism, 53–55
   as term, 46–49
Repair, of relationships, 178
Replacement "religion," 146
Republicanism, pro-Trump, 36
Restoring hope, 204–205
Reverse ABCDs, 169–172, 174–185
Revision-67, 66
Rituals, 99
Robertson, Pat, 105–106

Sacralization, moral, 152–153
Sartre, J.-P., 187
Schemas, 97–98
Science, mistrust of, 23
Secularity, 5, 74–75, 77–78, 189
Secularization hypothesis, 18–19
Secular spirituality, 74–75, 77–78
Security-focused beliefs, 149–151,
   203
Self-care, 172–174
Self-esteem, 111–113
Self spirituality, 194–195
September 11, 2001, events of, 105

The 700 Club, 105
Sexism, 23
Sexual abuse scandals, 24
Shame, 128–129
"Sick soul," 201–202
Significance, 109–110
Simplistic views, of suffering, 20–21,
   26–29
Social demands of the culture, 36
Social insularity, 146
Social support, 173
Spiritual but not religious, 79
Spirituality, 5, 34
   inclusive, 193
   nature, 193–194
   nonreligious, 193
   persistence of, 191–193
   postreligious. *See* Postreligious
      spirituality
   secular, 74–75, 77–78
   self, 194–195
   theistic, 193–194
   transcendent, 194
Spiritual narcissism, 53–55
Spiritual yearning, 195–196
Sprawling effect of religion, 91–93
Stagnation, cultural, 20–24
Starting points, 82
Strategic defensiveness, 107
Struggles, 64–65
Style of belief, as predictor of leaving,
   39
Suffering, 20–21, 26–29, 34
Superstition, 95
Support groups, 173
Survivors of abuse, 40
Symbolic immortality, 117–118

Taboo behaviors, 94
Theistic spirituality, 193–194
Theodicy, 27
Therapists, 57, 172–173
Tragedy, as predictor of leaving, 38
Transcendent connection, 120

Transcendent spirituality, 194
Trauma severity, as predictor of
    leaving, 39
Trump, Donald, 29–30. *See also*
    Pro-Trump Republicanism
Trust, 50–53, 203–204

Unbelief, 5
Uncertainty, 133–134

Values, 91–92, 160
Vulnerability, psychological, 49

Walking away from religion, 59–83
    changes after leaving religion, 74–80
    charting your course, 82–83
    distinct departures, 73–74
    reconstruction, 80–81
    religious deconstruction, 61–67
    religious deidentification, 67–73
    starting points, 59–61
Well-being of others, 180
White supremacy, 23
Women, 23
Worldviews, 119–121, 156–157, 172

ABOUT THE AUTHOR

Daryl Van Tongeren, PhD, is a professor of psychology at Hope College and the director of the Frost Center for Social Science Research. Trained as an experimental social psychologist, he has published more than 200 scholarly articles and chapters on topics such as religion, meaning in life, and virtues. His research has been covered by numerous media outlets, including the *New York Times*, *Chicago Tribune*, *Washington Post*, *The Atlantic*, NPR-affiliated radio stations, *Scientific American*, and *Men's Health*. This is his fourth book, authoring *The Complete Researcher* in 2023, *Humble* in 2022, and coauthoring *The Courage to Suffer* (with Sara A. Showalter Van Tongeren) in 2020. His work has been supported by numerous grants from the John Templeton Foundation, and he has won national and international awards for his research. He won the Margaret Gorman Early Career Award from APA's Division 36 (Psychology of Religion and Spirituality) in 2022 and the Early Career Contributions Award from the International Society for the Science of Existential Psychology. He also was named a 2016 Rising Star from the Association for Psychological Science (APS). He is a fellow of APS and the Society of Experimental Social Psychology. Currently, he is an associate editor for *The Journal of Positive Psychology* and a consulting editor for *Psychology of Religion and Spirituality* and the *Journal of Social Psychology*. He enjoys running, biking, and hiking near where he lives with his wife, Sara, in Holland, MI.